WHEN SINGAPORE FELL

By the same author

* A HISTORY OF MALAYA
* ASIAN NATIONALISM IN THE TWENTIETH CENTURY
* BRITISH CIVILIANS AND THE JAPANESE WAR IN
  MALAYA AND SINGAPORE, 1941–45

* *Also published by Macmillan*

When Singapore Fell

Evacuations and Escapes, 1941–42

Joseph Kennedy

Adult Education Tutor
University of Liverpool

MACMILLAN

First published 1989

Published by
THE MACMILLAN PRESS LTD
Houndmills, Basingstoke, Hampshire RG21 2XS
and London
Companies and representatives
throughout the world

Printed in Hong Kong

British Library Cataloguing in Publication Data
Kennedy, J. (Joseph), *date*
When Singapore fell: evacuations and
escapes, 1941–42.
1. Singapore. British civilians, Escapes,
1939–1945
I. Title
940.53'16
ISBN 0–333–45945–8

To the memory
of those who died on the way

Contents

List of Maps

List of Plates

Acknowledgements

Generous assistance towards the preparation of this book came from many sources. Mr Philip Reed, Deputy to the Keeper of the Department of Documents at the Imperial War Museum, made initial suggestions for the book and gave regular help and guidance subsequently. Members of the staff of the Documents and Printed Books Departments at the Museum were invariably courteous and helpful. Mr A. S. Bell and Mr A. Lodge, Librarian and Deputy Librarian at Rhodes House Library, Oxford, gave me every assistance again, as they have done previously. Commander A. Hague, of the Naval Historical Records Branch of the Ministry of Defence, and Mr Donald H. Simpson, Librarian of the Royal Commonwealth Society, provided me with every facility and encouragement to pursue my theme.

Other libraries or institutions which rendered assistance include the Library of the London School of Oriental and African Studies in the University of London; Manchester Central Library; the Picton Library, Liverpool; Lloyds Register of Shipping; and the Mapping and Charting Establishment R. E. at Tolworth.

Depositors and trustees of private papers listed in the Bibliography are especially thanked for allowing access to their documents and giving me permission to publish from them. Every effort has been made to trace all the copyright-holders but if any have been inadvertently overlooked the publishers will be pleased to make the necessary arrangement at the first opportunity.

Many correspondents, as listed, were generous in providing the benefit of their special knowledge and experience. A debt of gratitude is due to them and also to the authors of the many published works which have been consulted.

Mrs J. C. James has typed the text with her usual care and efficiency.

While recognising this large measure of assistance, the author must accept his sole responsibility for any errors or omissions.

JOSEPH KENNEDY

List of Abbreviations

AIF   Australian Imperial Forces
FMS   Federated Malay States
KMT   Kuomintang (Chinese Nationalist Party)
MCP   Malayan Communist Party
PWD   Public Works Department, Malaya
RAAF   Royal Australian Air Force
RAF   Royal Air Force (British)

Prologue

Large numbers of women and children were boarding ocean-going ships in Singapore. The British and their allies had withdrawn to the island and were to defend it, but in southern Malaya the Japanese army was already planning to cross the Johore Strait. In the short, fierce battle for Singapore which was to follow, the dangers, of both staying and leaving, grew daily. Most of the British and their allies were duty-bound to stay until the end, but more women and children would be shipped out in all kinds of small craft, and some military and civilian specialists would go too. Near to the time of the surrender of the island, on 15 February 1942, troops and civilians would make late, desperate efforts to get away. Small numbers still cut off on the Malayan mainland were looking for a way out by coast or through jungle. Evacuation, escape, death or capture; for most of those caught up in the surrender there would be little or no choice. For all, the immediate future would be painful and hazardous.

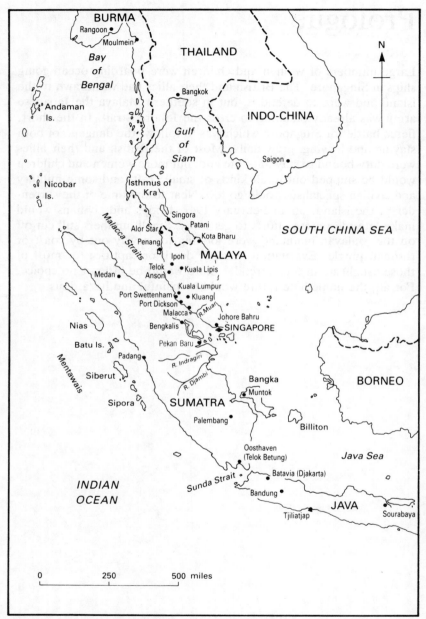

MAP 1 Malay Archipelago and Indian Ocean, 1941–42

1 Singapore, 1941–2

The military campaign which followed the Japanese invasion of Malaya in December 1941 was short and dramatic. In the space of eight weeks the Japanese army advanced from close to the Thai border to the southern tip of the Malay Peninsula. A week later, Japanese troops landed on Singapore island and scarcely another week had passed when, on 15 February 1942, Singapore formally surrendered to the Japanese commander.

Until a very late stage before the event, the Japanese invasion itself had been neither unexpected nor fully expected. Much the same could be said about the preparations for the defence of Malaya, which was a British responsibility. It was foreseen that Japan's recently gained control of the French colonial territories known collectively as 'Indo-China' provided bases from which a Japanese invasion force could mount a sea-borne attack on the north-east coast of Malaya, with landings also in southern Thailand, yet, in the event, the defence arrangements proved inadequate to check the invasion in the landing areas. One particular source of weakness was the lack of a political agreement or decision to allow British military leaders to send troops forward for the coastal defence of southern Thailand, where Japanese units landed with virtually no opposition.

There was much more to the military situation than the strategy of initial landing areas, though these were well chosen by the Japanese. From the first encounters the Japanese had superiority in both numbers and quality of aircraft to support the fighting on the ground. The great naval base at Singapore, which had been in the course of construction for most of 20 years, off and on, was complete, but the main British fleet which was to be based there was still in the process of preparation. Two capital ships sent out to 'show the flag', *Repulse* and *Prince of Wales*, headed northwards through the South China Sea to challenge the Japanese armada; both were sunk by suicidal dive-bombing. The sudden and total loss of these ships and the speed of the Japanese military advance overland towards the west coast of the peninsula to the north of Penang caused a great shock effect in Malaya, both in British military circles and among British civilian expatriates, and even more among the Malayan population as a whole. A British decision to abandon Penang and evacuate British

1

residents from the island sharpened the effect of everything else that
had happened by mid-December 1941.

Even in the briefest outline of the military campaign in Malaya in
1941–2, it must be recognised that the war which broke out in Europe
in September 1939 had made priority demands elsewhere on British
naval and military resources: on ships, aircraft, manpower and all
manner of stores and equipment. Among these priorities was the
despatch of war supplies of all kinds by a northern sea-route to the
Soviet Union during the late months of 1941, with its accompanying
toll of naval and merchant shipping. From the British point of view,
too, the entry of Mussolini's Italy into the war in 1940, in support of
Hitler's Germany, meant that shipping convoys carrying troops and
equipment for the Middle East theatre of war had to make the long
sea-voyage via the Cape and South Africa. In the event, the time
scale was such that ships, men and stores intended for the Middle
East were diverted, *en route*, to go to the aid of Singapore.

The Japanese military leadership was well aware of the incomplete
state of British naval defence based on Singapore and of the logistical
and other problems which Britain would face in sending reinforcements, even from the Middle East and India, to the Malayan zone.
The Japanese political–military decision to invade Malaya and plan a
bold, rapid campaign which would end in control of Singapore was a
feature of the same breathtaking opportunism as the simultaneous
and crushing Japanese air attack on the American Pacific Fleet at
Pearl Harbor. Beyond Pearl Harbor lay further prizes in the Pacific
and a view of the Australian continent. Beyond Singapore and to east
and west of this focal point in South-East Asia lay the Netherlands
East Indies, cut off by German victories from its European metropo-
lis and rich in many natural resources, including a precious war
commodity: oil.

In Malaya itself, there had been great efforts to help meet the
needs of Britain's efforts, especially in the key production industries
of tin and rubber. While the war was far away in Europe, economic
prosperity in Malaya, shared by all communities, may have helped to
promote a false sense of security. Some parents arranged for children
attending boarding school in England to come out to Malaya, where
they would be safer. In the light of Japan's recent record of military
aggression in China, especially southern China, there was serious
concern about the attitude and ambitions of the Tokyo government,
but also a widespread feeling that Malaya, including Singapore, was
safe enough. Either the Japanese advance would stop comfortably

3

MAP 2 Singapore, 1941–2

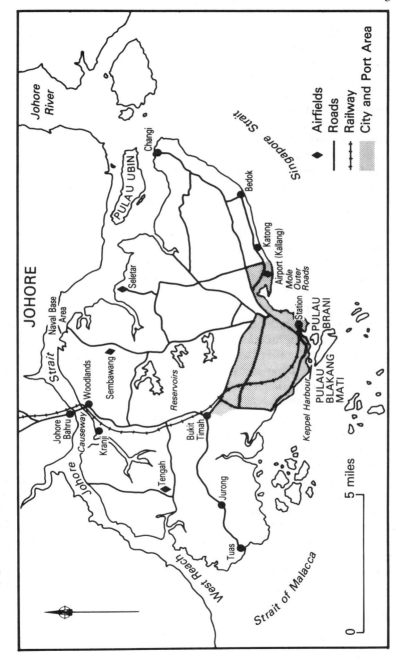

Airfields
Roads
Railway
City and Port Area

JOHORE

Johore River

PULAU UBIN

Changi

Bedok

Katong

Singapore Strait

Airport (Kallang)
*Mole
Outer
Roads*

Seletar

Naval Base Area

Station

PULAU BRANI

PULAU BLAKANG MATI

Keppel Harbour

Strait

Woodlands

Sembawang

Reservoirs

Johore Bahru

Causeway

Kranji

Bukit Timah

Tengah

Jurong

Tuas

West Reach

Strait of Malacca

0   5 miles

short of Malaya or, if war did come to Malayan territory, the invaders would be quickly driven off at well-prepared defence points. In all this kind of thought there was underestimation and overestimation. Underestimated was the level of Japanese ambition and the high morale and fighting qualities of troops well seasoned during the long period of warfare in China. Overestimated was the role of Singapore as an 'impregnable fortress', a 'bastion of the East'. This was a false representation. Singapore, in defence terms, was little more than a large naval base which required the operational presence of a substantial modern fleet and a large number of modern, effective aircraft. In December 1941, Singapore had neither of these resources but the myth of its 'strength' persisted almost to the very end.

The fighting in the Malay Peninsula took the form, partly, of direct infantry attacks by the Japanese, usually on a narrow front, sometimes accompanied by light tanks. Reconnaissance and fighter – bomber aircraft supplemented the ground fighting and smaller companies used jungle paths to infiltrate behind defensive lines. Along the coast, too, especially the west coast, boat-parties of soldiers moved from north to south, using river estuaries as bases for surprise lateral or pincer-type attack. The British and Allied response was to occupy prepared defensive positions, some of them only hastily prepared, until either driven back or at risk of being cut off by the more creative Japanese tactics. When this occurred, withdrawals took place to further chosen positions, often at a considerable distance further south. A series of defeats and withdrawals on the British side brought heavy casualties and an increasing loss of morale. British and Indian troops took the brunt of the defensive fighting in northern and central Malaya and among them were recent arrivals, some only partly trained. On the other side, a quickly established command of the air meant that Japanese field commanders received intelligence information of a kind far superior to that which reached their British counterparts, who were at times almost 'working in the dark'. Although there were acts of bravery by individuals and small groups among the defenders, only the Argyll and Sutherland Highlanders earned a firm reputation as jungle fighters in the long withdrawal from northern Malaya. On 7 January 1942, the Japanese broke through a defensive line once again, this time at Slim River in Perak, and yet another extensive stretch of territory was left open to them, including Kuala Lumpur, capital of the Federated Malay States, and the towns of Malacca, Kuala Pilah and Seremban.

Further north, the important towns of Ipoh, Taiping and Kuala Kangsar had already fallen under Japanese control.

General Percival, officer-in-charge of Malaya Command, and General Wavell, newly appointed Supreme Commander of a whole region of South-East Asia and the south-west Pacific, now agreed on a further defensive line, approximately matching the northern boundary of the state of Johore. Australian troops, many of them recent arrivals at Singapore, were given an important role to play here, under their own commander, General Gordon-Bennett. There was some hard and bitter fighting, but, in essentials, the pattern of events remained the same. Withdrawals brought new problems. Guns were pulled back so that they would not fall into the hands of the Japanese, and then infantry units were recalled because they lacked the support of the guns. One reorganized defence followed another, and always the movement was nearer to Singapore. Less than three weeks after the Slim River battle in central Malaya, General Percival warned Wavell that the situation in Johore was critical and, on 28 January, he ordered a complete withdrawal to the island of Singapore by 31 January. When this was accomplished, the causeway joining Johore to the island was breached by explosives and the scene was set for the final episode of the Malayan Campaign: the battle for Singapore itself.

Civilian refugees, mostly Europeans at first, had been making their way to Singapore, as best they could, from 'the north' and 'up-country' for many weeks before the last stage of the war in Malaya was reached. Towards the end of January 1942, the numbers of refugees increased dramatically. Both military and civilian refugees were evident as remnants of army units made their way to the island alongside a flood of civilians of many races, but predominantly Asian now. For all of them, regardless of category or race, the one hope of escaping life under Japanese military occupation was that, somehow, Singapore would live up to its 'fortress' reputation and hold out. General Wavell, too, thought that the island should be able to hold out for some months and allow further reinforcements and aircraft to arrive. Troops and military stores and equipment were still arriving in ships docking at Singapore even into the early days of February 1942, though by this time both the RAF and the navy were beginning to plan in terms of withdrawal from the island. A small group of British army officers was engaged in planning a possible 'escape route' through the archipelago, south of Singapore, to eastern Sumatra and from there overland to Padang on the west coast. Food dumps were being arranged to assist such a movement.

Given the speed of the Japanese advance down the Malay Peninsula and the related British and Allied hopes that the attack would be held back at some defensive position – Jitra in the north, or the Slim River front in central Malaya, or on the line roughly marking the Johore northern boundary in the south – it is not surprising that any limited plans to evacuate civilian or military personnel in the event of a Japanese victory were formulated only at a late stage. While British expatriate women and children were generally ordered south ahead of military withdrawals, they normally reached Singapore through the use of family cars, sometimes shared, and the hospitality of friends found *en route*. Some travelled on trains and found recently appointed civil officers trying to sort out evacuee problems as people moved hurriedly south. In the city of Singapore itself, there was a major billeting problem for people who had come down from Malaya, but the position was helped greatly by individual offers of shelter and hospitality. Many of those still there at the last stages of the fighting were sheltering in the basements of hotels and public buildings in central Singapore.

Expatriate families, mainly British, had difficult choices to make. Some made an early choice and sea passages to Australia from Singapore were booked for many women and children over a period of months before the Japanese invasion of Malaya. Others held on, to stay together as long as possible; many hoped, in any case, that the threat of war would recede. Many British women were working in the voluntary services; British men were mostly part-time trained soldiers in the Volunteers, or were Reservists, or exempted by virtue of their employment in essential services. Older men were recruited in local and civil defence units and all British males up to the age of 55 were liable for public duties. The early departures of some women and children had to some extent reduced the size of the British civilian expatriate community in Malaya and Singapore, but there would have been little recent shift on the men's side in the period shortly before the Japanese invasion. There is evidence that some children attending boarding school in England were brought out from England for their greater safety, in what was seen as the 'European war'. Some others even returned from Australia.

The possibility of a mainland retreat in Malaya in the face of a serious enemy invasion from the north was certainly recognised, especially with a view to gaining time for army, air force and navy reinforcements to arrive at Singapore. When the island of Penang was left without defence forces, only a week after the initial Japanese landings on the east coast of the Malay Peninsula, the British navy began to make early contingency plans for a possible staged with-drawal from the great naval base in Singapore. The movement of civilians from battle areas took place according to circumstances and under the orders of the military leaders. There was little or no earlier planning here and most European women and children, together with some of the older men, made their way south, to become refugees in Singapore. As the Japanese army advanced, the flow of refugees was joined by a large number of Asian civilians, especially from the time when the main fighting area became centred in Johore.

By January 1942, the number of people living on Singapore island, mainly in and around the city area, was approaching one million, about double the normal figure. Including troops, there may have been almost another half-million on the island when the surrender took place in mid-February. When retreating soldiers and desperate civilians made for the island, war casualties in Singapore began to take a serious toll of the population. As the Japanese hold on the Malay Peninsula increased, so did the frequency and intensity of air attacks on Singapore by planes which had shorter flights and a quicker turn-around from nearer air bases. At first, the main targets of the bombing aircraft were the army, navy and air force bases, but soon, the docks, warehouses, railway station and down-town living areas were under frequent attack. Among the urban Chinese of Singapore the loss of life from aerial attack was particularly heavy and tragic. Large mass graves had to be hastily dug for the victims. At the same time, the hospitals in Singapore were crammed full with both military and civilian casualties.

'European' sectors of Singapore did not escape damage and deaths. They suffered first from bombing and then from the shelling from the Malayan mainland which followed. British civilian resi-dents, already harbouring in their houses refugees from 'the north' and 'up-country' began to move, with their emergency guests, into the cellars and basements of public buildings in the city centre and take up a squatter- type existence, holding on to the few possessions they had been able to carry there. Some were compelled to move because of the presence of guns on sites adjacent to their own houses,

which created great noise and blast effect and were liable to draw
Japanese fire in reply. Bomb-blast, too, and shrapnel from shell-fire
were sources of great danger to squatting refugees; the latter, particularly, appearing to penetrate anywhere. Along the line of a waterfront which had been built up on land recovered from coastal swamp,
tropical drain-ditches served as some kind of immediate personal
protection but the low level of land above water had, at the time,
been considered too much of a problem there for any significant
provision of air-raid shelters.

After the Johore causeway was breached on 31 January, troops were
allocated positions for the defence of the island of Singapore. The
plan was the obvious one of sharply repulsing any invasion attempt,
but, in retrospect, the criticism was made that the north-west corner
of the island should have been allocated a greater concentration of
defending troops. It was in this region that the main Japanese attack
took place. Following heavy air attacks and a sustained artillery
barrage, Japanese troops landed in the night and early morning of 8/9
February. It was soon obvious that they had gained a significant
bridgehead, about three miles wide, despite the difficulties of pen-
etrating a swampy coastline. Japanese military commanders had
calculated that they had more to gain than to lose by striking quickly
after winning control of the peninsula. The process of retreat had
demoralised some of the British and Allied defenders, among whom
there were many who were unseasoned and not yet acclimatised.
Many had arrived only in time for the last two weeks of the fighting in
Malaya. Others landed too late even to reach the Malayan mainland.
Ships which had brought in large numbers of late troop reinforcements to Singapore left hurriedly, packed with women and children
evacuees who were leaving at the eleventh hour. Only three or four
days before Japanese troops landed on Singapore, big ships were still
arriving at the port with troops, military equipment and stores. They
left with evacuees as late as 6 February, and these were not the last.
Mostly in much smaller vessels of all kinds, women and children,
selected army, navy and RAF personnel, and technically qualified
civilians, sailed south from Singapore at different dates and times
between 10 and 15 February.

This was a late evacuation in a situation of great peril, both at the docks and at sea. As events would prove, for many it would have been much safer to have stayed behind than to have sailed. On 10 February, it was reported that the Japanese were already in control of the naval base, where much destruction of equipment and stores, including oil, had been taking place. By this date, the navy was preparing to evacuate Singapore and all auxiliary naval vessels had orders to prepare for sea. Rear-Admiral Spooner, senior naval officer at Singapore, informed General Wavell that he intended to carry out a naval evacuation on 11 February. Some who knew about this still appeared to regard the situation as being a temporary setback rather than a symbol of a major defeat.

There was no question of trying to evacuate a large army contingent of about 80 000 troops, or even a majority of the European civilians still on the island. When the island was surrendered four days later, most of these faced imprisonment or internment. There was, however, official concern to try to evacuate women and children and, among the women, nursing sisters from the hospitals. On a very limited scale, armed forces personnel and male civilians with specialist knowledge were selected for evacuation on the grounds that they could continue to contribute to the war effort elsewhere, in India, for example, or Ceylon or Burma. In this latter category were Harbour Board and Railways officials and officers of the Public Works Department from Malaya. Many RAF and navy personnel, with no further useful role to play in Singapore were directed southwards also, with the island of Java as the main initial objective of a great flotilla of ships and boats which left Singapore in the last three or four days before the British surrender.

In the words of a naval report relating to Singapore on the morning of 11 February, the situation was 'most confused from now on'. Among chaotic scenes at the docks, where Japanese bombing and shelling were almost continuous, all kinds of overloaded craft sailed out. Some were in approximately convoy formation and accompanied by naval, or auxiliary naval craft; others, more haphazardly, went forward in small numbers, or even independently, as best they could, according to time and circumstance. All had to find a way through minefields and face the grave dangers of Japanese air attacks through the daylight hours. Some evacuee vessels came to be confronted by a squadron of the Japanese surface fleet, part of a task-force operating in the Bangka Strait.

In the land-fighting on the island of Singapore the story of Japanese success continued. Far from being a fortress, Singapore proved to be an island difficult to defend against determined, well-organised invaders. With the assistance of artillery shelling and constant aerial support, Japanese infantry pressed forward from their main landing areas in the north-west of the island towards the hilly central region of Bukit Timah, which housed the island's main water reservoirs. These reservoirs were supplementary to a piped water-supply carried across the causeway from Johore; a causeway quickly repaired by the Japanese and held in their control. The British and Allied military forces on Singapore were numerically much larger than those of the Japanese invasion force but their numbers were to count for little. It was held later that they had been too widely spread and suffered from weaknesses in communication, especially in the north-west and west of the island. Again, as often in Malaya, tactical withdrawals were demoralising and air defence was lacking. There was some brave defensive fighting by British and Allied troops and a Malay regiment also fought with distinction. A strong fighting spirit, too, was evident in the ranks of a large Chinese volunteer force assembled towards the end of the campaign in the Peninsula, but the Chinese were short on training and equipment. By 13 February, this force had been disbanded to avoid a situation in which many Chinese might have become prisoners when clearly bearing arms against the Japanese.

An Australian war correspondent recalled later that, as early as 10 February, most of those in close touch with the situation realised that the fall of Singapore lay only a few days away. As naval vessels and naval personnel became no longer useful in Singapore the plan was to withdraw them to Java, but a priority aim was also to ship out any remaining RAF personnel, together with their stores and equipment where possible. Between 11 and 14 February, a whole range of shipping, most of it consisting of small vessels, and among them many naval auxiliaries, was leaving docks and quaysides at Singapore and heading south. This was, of necessity, a somewhat hasty and improvised operation, but yet characterised by certain general features. Priority in evacuation was given to women and children and to certain categories and quotas of servicemen and of civilian technical staffs. Inevitably, under pressure of hasty departures, often in highly dangerous situations, nothing was as clear-cut as all this might suggest.

Despite the presence of military police on guard duties at dock gates, the issuing of passes and other efforts towards the maintenance of a controlled operation, there must often have seemed to be more chaos than order about what was happening. From 11 February onwards there were many wandering groups of soldiers in the city and docks area, some with little or no discipline left, ready to attempt to force their way on to evacuating vessels, if and where they saw a chance to do so. Through much of the daytime, bombing and shelling continued in the docks area and a thick pall of smoke from burning oil depots and other storage centres created a scene of terror and near despair, 'like Dante's *Inferno*', as one witness recalled. Meanwhile, the land-fighting was coming closer and closer towards the city itself. Further Japanese landings were reported from west of Changi on the night of 12/13 February and, about the same time, there was said to be heavy Japanese pressure on the road between Bukit Timah and the outer reaches of the city, including Tanglin.

General Percival called a final conference on the morning of 15 February. Japanese troops now held Bukit Timah and the island's reservoirs. From that vantage point they could direct artillery fire down upon the city. The decision to be made was either for a counter-attack to dislodge the Japanese from their positions, secure the water-supply provided by the reservoirs and re-take a number of nearby supply dumps, or to surrender, in the hope of sparing the city, with its swollen population of more than a million people, from the horrors of warfare. To counter-attack and fail might lead to the worst possible outcome, so the conference turned its attention to the theme of surrender. By this time, the word 'capitulation' was entering into rumours in Singapore, though there were other stories of further reinforcements, including American help, approaching the island. At last, a message began to circulate that anyone able to find a way off the island without prejudice to the rights of others was free to do so. Not all would hear this and comparatively few, in any case, were in a position to respond.

Following the military surrender by General Percival on 15 February 1942, Sir Shenton Thomas, the civil governor of Singapore, and Lady Thomas became internees, the governor shortly being moved further east to Formosa and then Manchuria. Other senior administrators from the colonial government were interned in Changi gaol and some of them died there. General Percival, Brigadier Ivan Simson, lately responsible for civil defence, and most British and Allied military leaders became prisoners-of-war, together with the vast majority of the troops who had served under them. Only the existence of a late escape route via islands to the south had some notable effect on reducing the number of soldiers captured at Singapore. Part-time soldiers in Volunteers' units became military prisoners if they were in uniform; some of them were civilians who had been on government service leave in Australia when the Japanese attacked Malaya. Returning as quickly as possible, they had just a week or two back in Singapore before entering a prison camp. Like other part-time soldiers, they were liable to be sent to the notorious railway construction camps in Thailand and Sumatra.

A handful of very senior officers took part in evacuation or escape moves. The Australian General Gordon-Bennett reached Sumatra and flew back to his homeland. It was a controversial decision and one about which he later wrote in defence of his own action. Less controversial was the attempt at escape undertaken by Rear-Admiral Spooner in the company of Air Vice-Marshal Pulford, senior RAF officer and Air Officer Commanding Far East. Both the RAF and the navy were officially withdrawing from Singapore before the end. There were no safe airfields in Malaya or Singapore left to the RAF and many aircraft had been lost in combat or destroyed on the ground. The navy had begun to evacuate the large naval base on the north side of Singapore by the time the land war in Malaya had reached southern Johore, and much demolition work was carried out there. Not until nearly midnight on 13 February did the Admiral and Air Vice-Marshal leave Singapore in the launch, *Fairmile*, in the company of some 40 other servicemen, the majority from the navy and the Marines. The vessel was crowded, there were almost immediate problems with the steering and they were grounded on a reef until carried off by a rising tide. It was an inauspicious start to an ill-fated voyage. For most of that day (14 February), they anchored by a small group of islands, and on the Sunday, the day when Singapore surrendered, they reached the Puloh Tujoh group of islands, some 30 miles to the east of Bangka. One of the naval officers, Lieutenant R. A. Pool, had badly damaged his fingers and the Admiral was concerned to try to reach Muntok and a doctor.

In the account given later by Lieutenant I. W. Stonor of the Argyll and Sutherland Highlanders, formerly ADC to General Percival, *Fairmile* sighted a formation of Japanese cruisers ahead and made back with all possible speed to the shelter of the islands. There followed a chase and shell-fire from a Japanese destroyer as well as a diving attack from a Japanese seaplane, which was driven off by fire from AA twin Lewis guns. But *Fairmile* ran aground on a shoal near a large village, and its occupants swam or waded to the beach. Four officers stayed with the launch and faced a Japanese landing party from the destroyer who ordered them ashore in a dinghy before removing charts and putting the engines of the launch out of action. Next morning, *Fairmile* was machine-gunned and bombed again on the shoal and its crew and passengers were left shipwrecked and isolated, with only the ship's dinghy. It remained to be seen whether any of the Malay boats left behind by villagers, who had mostly left the island of Chulia in the best of their boats the day before, could be repaired sufficiently to be seaworthy.

One boat was prepared and provisioned for a voyage to Batavia, where further help would be sought. In charge was a naval lieutenant, and with him two Javanese who had been attached to the island's wireless station. Acting on previous orders, the staff of the wireless station had destroyed everything that mattered when, from their hill top position, they had first sighted Japanese ships. No news came back from the Batavia venture and a further rescue mission by two staff sergeants of the Royal Engineers in a boat with islander Malays was also unsuccessful.

According to Lieutenant Stonor the shipwrecked party was never wholly short of food. They had salvaged supplies from the launch and found fruit and rice on the island. Local Malays, coming and going in boats to rescue some of their belongings, were able to supply fish, and there were chickens and turtle eggs to be found. More-serious problems arose through a change of diet, change of weather and, perhaps above all, the psychological pressures on marooned men. The island was a mile long and a quarter of a mile wide. It was very malarial and when the rainy season started many of the men suffered from chills and fevers. They began to die, many giving up hope that they would ever be rescued. There was no doctor with the party and 19 deaths were recorded between mid-February and mid-May 1942. Among the victims were the Rear-Admiral, the Air Vice-Marshal and a senior naval officer, Commander Frampton.

As the rest of this story moves in scene and time further from Singapore, it must be summarised briefly. With great efforts, the survivors worked to prepare another Malay boat for the sea, the work commencing under Commander Frampton and continuing after his death under Lieutenant Pool. On 13 May, they set sail northwards for the island of Sya, but foundered eventually on some rocks close by. With the help of a Malay fishing boat, and after some further delay, the survivors from Chulia were taken to the island of Singkep. They were met by Javanese police wearing Japanese badges. Such as it had been, their period of freedom, lasting about three months, was over, but at least there was hospital treatment on Singkep before events turned full circle and they were taken back to Singapore and Changi prison, arriving there in early June.

———————

The crews of merchant ships moving in and out of Singapore in January and early February 1942 faced fearful situations. Theirs is a story which has never been adequately told, but an account by Captain Michael J. Curtis, who served at the time as a midshipman on the Blue Funnel cargo liner, *Talthybius*, provides some sharp insights. A ship of more than 10 000 tons gross, *Talthybius* was designed for world trade and soon called into war service. Part of a large convoy of some 50 ships, *Talthybius* left Liverpool at the end of September 1941 and called at Cardiff and Swansea for coaling purposes and the loading of army vehicles, equipment and stores. Then it was out to the Atlantic for the long sea-journey via South Africa to the Middle East. The ship had a complement of 77 men, 22 of them British merchant navy officers and the rest Chinese, who filled the roles from bosun downwards. *Talthybius* carried guns mounted for her own defence and a team of 11 gunners. The Maritime Anti-Aircraft Regiment of the Royal Artillery (a unit which appears to have had little publicity) provided eight of the gunners, two others were merchant seamen and there was one leading seaman gunner from the Royal Navy. As they steamed along the eastern seaboard of South Africa towards Durban, they learned of the Japanese attacks on Pearl Harbor and Malaya and were not surprised when new instructions came though to proceed to Bombay. Here, *Talthybius* joined a convoy bound for Singapore via Ceylon.

In two lines, the convoy headed, via Sunda and Bangka, to the Western Roads at Singapore. On the afternoon of 25 January 1942, *Talthybius* moved into the western wharf of Keppel Harbour and began unloading cargo. Ships were still coming and going and dock labour was still available. In the course of the next three days, by dint of working round the clock, dock labour discharged the cargo carried by *Talthybius*, except for a great quantity of coal brought in the holds. Unloading of this coal commenced on 29 January.

Air raids, which had at first been spasmodic and intermittent in character, began now to follow a regular pattern as the docks became a prime target for the Japanese bombers. Unloading was interrupted by the bombing and the local dock labour force melted away. The work soon stopped altogether and the coal had to remain largely on the ship as *Talthybius* moved to the main wharf and awaited further orders. On 30 January, the new orders were received. A cargo of airstrip construction material was to be loaded next day, part of the equipment of a unit operated by the New Zealand Air Force. The cargo and the New Zealanders were to be taken to Telok Betong (Dutch, Oosthaven) in southern Sumatra. The machinery began to arrive that evening, but, next morning, there was no dock labour to load it. Work could only be commenced after the four midshipmen on *Talthybius* had instructed the New Zealand team 'in the art of handling ships' derricks and driving steam winches'; local labour had simply disappeared. On 3 February, as a final piece of machinery was being swung into position, 27 Japanese bombers, approaching from the north, passed directly over the ship and bombs fell unpleasantly close. Returning on the same bearing, they made directly for *Talthybius*, dropping bombs on and around her with ear-splitting explosions.

On the fore deck, smoke billowed from No. 2 hatchway, where the last of the machinery was being loaded. A New Zealand warrant officer was killed outright and six other men, including a ship's gunner, were severely burned by flames caused by bombs falling on vehicles with full fuel tanks and standing on a floor of coal. All that afternoon, the ship's crew fought the fires, only to discover that near-misses on the starboard side had severely damaged the hull with shrapnel, and water was pouring into the stoke-hold and engine-room. By the time the fire was finally extinguished, the ship was listing badly to starboard and 'obviously settling on the uneven bottom of Keppel Harbour'. The task now was to get the ship afloat as soon as possible and into dry dock and for this the assistance of a diver and salvage pumps were essential. Great efforts were made in the next few days, though the bombing raids became even more frequent. It was at this juncture that the *Empress of Asia*, a 17 000-ton ship bringing in troops and equipment, was bombed and set on fire in Singapore Harbour, ending as a blackened hulk. About the same time, a massive pall of smoke from the northern side of the island could only mean that the great naval base near Seletar had either been hit or had been deliberately set on fire to deny the use of its installations to the Japanese.

Captain Curtis has recalled in remarkable detail the continued efforts to float *Talthybius* and move her from the Main Wharf to the more sheltered waters of the Empire Dock. This was achieved on 7 February, but pumping was still necessary and when a fault developed in one of the pumps, the ship 'settled back on the bottom again'. The assistance of a diver and his squad was again awaited while the midshipmen continued to rig staging and prepare timber bungs. A stick of bombs from a sudden air raid killed one of the ship's stewards, caught in the open and carrying water from the cold storage depot, as they had been doing for days. That night came the heavy and continuous sound of an artillery barrage and, next day (9 February), rumours circulated that the Japanese had landed on the island. But when the diver turned up again, the efforts to plug and rescue the ship continued. The next experience of the ship's crew was to be under artillery fire, with shells whistling overhead, punctuated by the increasing pressure of aerial attacks on the port area. Transit sheds on the wharf alongside the ship were set on fire and fire-fighting became an immediate priority to stop the flames spreading to the ship itself. By now, it was too dangerous to carry out further diving work, but the pumps were slowly reducing the level of water in the ship. It was a good sign, but it was going to need time. The shells were flying overhead between guns stationed on the island of Blakang Mati and Japanese gun positions somewhere to the north. All seemed to be getting uncomfortably close and the few ships still left in Keppel Harbour moved out on the evening of 10 February, with Europeans on board. There were rumours about a general evacuation.

The Master of *Talthybius* would not approve a hurried plan to fuel and provision a small tug, abandoned by its crew, for emergency use as a getaway vessel. No one would, at this stage, have his permission to leave until Naval Control issued instructions. The *Empire Star*, the largest ship seen in the port for some days, berthed at the Main Wharf on 11 February and immediately started to embark evacuees. Everyone now realised that the situation was desperate. No Chinese member of the crew of *Talthybius* had been seen for three or four days and the Master called together what was left of the ship's company. It was now, he said, a case of every man for himself. He would remain with the ship and the 3rd officer and 2nd steward said they would remain with him; the rest, seeing that no more could be done for the ship, decided to leave. They made first for the *Empire Star*, but, on the way, noticed a small ship flying the White Ensign and explained their position to the officer in charge. He accepted them on board and sent one of his sub-lieutenants to tell the Master of *Talthybius* he had come from Naval Control with orders for him to abandon. The Master and the two officers with him were to be brought back to join the others, on what was to become their rescue vessel. It was HMS *Ping Wo*, a pre-war Yangste river steamer, 200 feet long and with a shallow draft of only about six feet. Certainly not designed for the open seas, this little ship had been engaged on naval patrol work with a crew of local Chinese and Malay ratings. These now went ashore and the men from *Talthybius* willingly agreed to work their passage and get the ship away. Their casualties had been a Chinese steward killed, a seaman gunner badly burned and a 1st radio officer injured ashore during an air raid a few days previously, who had to be left in hospital, not fit to travel.

Working parties coaled the ship and helped themselves to food supplies from the transit sheds. By mid-afternoon, 11 February, *Ping Wo* was on the move to the Eastern Roads where, in the next few hours, nearly 200 Europeans and Eurasians, mostly civilians, were picked up as they came out in all manner of small boats from Clifford Pier. After dark, they headed south, making first for Java, where the civilian evacuees were transferred to other sea-going ships. There followed further coaling and provisioning and the *Ping Wo* set off for Australia. A disabled Australian destroyer had been in Singapore for refit and then towed to Batavia. Now, this ship, HMAS *Vendetta*, was towed by *Ping Wo*, which rolled at an average speed of five knots for the next 17 days. If it was extremely uncomfortable on *Ping Wo*, it must have been even worse on *Vendetta*, but both managed to reach Fremantle on 4 March. By now, the Japanese conquest of the Netherlands East Indies was almost complete.

All crew members of *Talthybius* were found billets with families in and around Fremantle and they experienced much kindness and hospitality. In turn, starting with the Master, the officers were shipped back to England; by July 1942 all were safely back. Meanwhile, in Singapore, the Japanese raised *Talthybius* and passed her into service under the name *Taruyasu Maru*; at the end of the war she was located in the Japanese port of Maizuru. Renamed again, *Empire Evenlode*, the ship was directed westwards under a new crew and with a full cargo of scrap-iron. There were serious problems with machinery and boilers and the long sea route via the Cape was chosen, with a protracted stay in Capetown to replace boiler tubes.

Finally, in May 1946, *Talthybius* (now *Empire Evenlode*) was back in Swansea once more, five years after the wartime departure for the

Middle East, and five months after leaving Japan. A survey of the
ship was undertaken and it was concluded that she was no longer fit
for service at sea. Sent to the shipbreakers, *Empire Evenlode* closely
followed the destiny of the load of scrap-iron which she had brought
all the way from the Far East!

The last days before the surrender of Singapore, on 15 February
1942, left strong visual impressions with all who witnessed the scenes.
There were fierce fires in many dockside warehouses and among the
shipping in the harbour. The smoke and fumes of burning dumps also
filled the air; some of this was due to the effects of Japanese bombing
and shelling, but much arose also from the deliberate destruction of
stores and supplies, especially oil installations. Like a great symbol of
doom, a heavy pall of smoke hung at times over the city and other
parts of the island. Attacking Japanese planes came over regularly,
while the artillery shelling became almost constant and from ever-
closer range. Military and civilian casualties packed the hospitals, the
dead being hastily buried in mass graves and ditches. Stocks of liquor
were being destroyed on government orders and normal commercial
business was rapidly closing down. The dockside was littered with
vehicles of all kinds and in all conditions, most suffering from the
effects of bombing and shrapnel. In places, cars were deliberately
pushed into the sea.

Those who sailed out of the port just before the end of the fighting
could still see, for a long period, the fires and smoke which they had
left behind. Many passed close to islands which told their own story
of destruction, especially Pulau Brani, with the thick black smoke
pouring from its great oil refinery.

It was against this nightmarish backcloth that late evacuees and
escapers left the stricken island and city of Singapore in February
1942. They were only a small fraction of the number of people left
behind, not only in Singapore, but also in Malaya, where some
soldiers and expatriate civilians were still operating behind Japanese
lines, while others, who had been cut off, were captured and held in
mainland prisons. Small groups of British and Allied troops and
civilians, including a number of former planters, tin-mine managers
and district officers, still moved in a kind of twilight freedom around

the jungle fringes. A few found the coast and left in small boats, but, for most, further freedom would depend on links with jungle-based guerilla units, mainly formed and led by young Chinese. Theirs was no more than partial 'escape', entailing many further challenges to survival.

2 Big Ships, Ocean Bound

Four big passenger liners, serving as wartime troopships, arrived in Singapore docks on 29 January 1942. They carried troops of the 18th Division and military equipment and stores in what was a late attempt to reinforce the defences of Malaya and Singapore. Troopships from Britain to the Middle East in 1941 had to make the long sea-journey via South Africa, and Churchill had been concerned to provide substantial additional forces, up to two infantry divisions, to be at hand for whatever developed in the Middle East theatre of war. With heavy demands on British merchant shipping, he secured the loan of six fast American merchant ships for this large-scale and long-distance kind of trooping, though, before Pearl Harbor, the American President thought it undesirable to send American ships directly into British waters. For the one division that was transported on the long sea voyage in 1941 before Pearl Harbor, British troops were first taken westward across the Atlantic to Halifax, Nova Scotia, then transferred to a convoy, known as WS 12X, which followed a wide route to South Africa, heading for the Cape and, eventually, the Red Sea.

While the ships of convoy WS 12X were still at sea the war changed dramatically, with the Japanese attacks on Pearl Harbor and Malaya. The main convoy was ordered to Bombay, where a new grouping, referred to as BM 11, sailed out for Singapore on 19 January 1942. Making south and east via Ceylon, these ships carried troops and military equipment which military leaders were hoping would help stem the Japanese advance in the Malay Peninsula. Altogether, this convoy carried nearly 12 000 troops in four large ships. The *Empress of Japan* (later re-named *Empress of Scotland*) and the *Duchess of Bedford*, normally Canadian Pacific liners, were now serving as wartime troopers, each carrying about 2000 troops. USS *Wakefield* and USS *West Point* were large American ships, recently loaned to Britain for troop movements; *Wakefield* had nearly 4500 troops on board and *West Point* carried 3250. With the big passenger liners sailed a cargo – passenger ship, *Empire Star*, carrying stores and equipment. Although it was never part of their original mission, all these ships, when emptied of troops, were to play a prominent part in the evacuation of women and children from Singapore. None of this could be clearly foreseen as they carried out their duties of trooping

20

and transporting military supplies. British naval ships provided a rota of escort duty between Bombay and Colombo, and Colombo and Singapore.

Convoy BM 11 reached Singapore Harbour on 28 January 1942, and docked next day. By this time the harbour area was a daily target for Japanese bombing planes and ships were in very grave danger. There was every reason to move quickly and troops were disembarked overnight and military cargoes unloaded as quickly as possible. The newly arrived soldiers, some of them only partly trained and all needing to acclimatise, faced a beleaguered situation in Singapore, where the causeway to the Johore mainland would be cut in two days time. Whilst unloading of the ships continued, lines of women and children were conducted aboard ships which showed plenty of evidence of ten days at sea in overcrowded conditions. In a situation of frequent bombing attacks the need to turn round with all speed was only too apparent and lighters continued with the work of unloading after the ships had left the dockside.

For the bigger ships, a system of booking passages through shipping offices appears to have persisted throughout. Doris Pelton, whose husband was to become a prisoner-of-war in Malaya and Thailand, worked as a civil defence ambulance driver in Kuala Lumpur. Withdrawn further south, at half-an-hour's notice, she reached Singapore and was housed by friends there, while her husband remained on military duties, somewhere 'up-country'. On 29 January 1942, Mrs Pelton was informed that there would be ships to take women and children away and tickets could be obtained from a shipping office from 9 p.m. that evening. On arrival there, she found 'a great crowd' and someone was shouting, 'Those for Colombo, go right. Those for United Kingdom, go left.' After a considerable wait, Doris Pelton came away from the office with a typewritten ticket, indicating space on a ship for one two-foot mattress. Embarkation would be on the next day and the issuing officer advised women to take their own dishes and cutlery.

Giles Playfair later described the temporary shipping office as 'a private house, situated in splendid isolation' in the neighbourhood of the botanical gardens. Part of the long drive to the house was barricaded to restrict the number of cars which could be parked there. An armed sentry was on duty and long queues formed. In this corner of what had been comfortable, suburban Singapore, major family and individual decisions were being made. None at the time could assess the risks of sailing and none could assess the nature and length of periods of separation between husbands and wives consequent on the tenure of a small paper ticket collected in Cluny Road. Some separations were permanent.

Not everyone succeeded in obtaining a ticket and some people found themselves returning again to the issuing office. On 30 January, Mr. A. E. Fawcett, an officer of the Federated Malay States Railways, accompanied his wife to Cluny Road, seeking a passage for her on the *Empress of Japan*. They were told it was 'impossible'; presumably someone had determined a deadline of timing or numbers. This made a decision for Dorothy Fawcett, who, like so many other women at the time, was caught in two minds and really preferred to stay. A few days later, however, she narrowly escaped death, or at least serious injury, when a bomb fell very close to the house in which she was living, bringing the ceilings down. Badly shaken, she was persuaded to leave later on a Free French ship, the *Felix Roussel*. Among other women passengers leaving on this ship was Mrs Marjorie Hudson, whose husband Tim, heavily engaged in air-raid precautions work, had helped to dig her out from below three dead bodies in a bomb-hole, as narrated by Noel Barber. She, too, was a reluctant evacuee.

Mrs Pelton had found deck-space on the *Duchess of Bedford* and acquired a mattress. Meanwhile, Mrs Dora Gurney, wife of a British headmaster in Malaya, was seeking a passage for herself and their three young children. She later recalled 'huge crowds' at the shipping offices; many were asked to leave a telephone number and told they would be informed when a ship came in. When the big liners came in, she was given a time by which to be at the docks and the instruction that passengers were only allowed one small case each. She and the children had only mattresses in the between-decks area of the *Empress of Japan* at first, but were later found a single-berth cabin for the four of them and considered themselves very lucky.

There was congestion and confusion as cars, taxis and lorries converged at the docks. As many vehicles were forced to make a long detour to avoid the dangers of unexploded bombs, long traffic lines built up. An air-raid alert was sounded in the middle of the afternoon of 30 January, but, fortunately, the bombers struck elsewhere this time. By 8 p.m. that evening, the *Empress of Japan* had completed the embarkation of passengers and was soon on the move to an outer anchorage, where it continued to unload Indian army military supplies into lighters. Meanwhile, the dockside warehouses were heavily bombed and set on fire. In the early morning (31 January), the two

American liners moved out and the Canadian Pacific ships followed a little later in the day. They carried anti-aircraft guns, which were soon in action against high-level bombing, and passengers were not allowed on deck until it was felt that comparative safety had been reached. The big ships kept a good speed of 18 knots in the open sea.

Conditions on board the evacuee ships were crowded and uncomfortable during the early stages of these voyages. At Singapore, there had been neither time nor opportunity to clean up the troop decks so hastily vacated. Most women and children endured a complete lack of privacy but their common situation brought them together in more senses than one. Dora Gurney recalled that, soon 'the women took over, and were quite marvellous, some in the galley, looking after the food, others cleaning-up in the bathrooms, etc. . . . The children were formed into groups and teachers held their classes.' Surgeon-Commander D. R. Goodfellow RN, a member of the naval medical staff on board, made his report in similar vein.

'The evacuees,' he wrote, 'adapted themselves to their new environment with commendable good humour and cooperation. Within a few hours of embarkation, the ship's own staff and military officers in charge of troops worked out a complete organisation for victualling, washing, hygiene, accommodation for nursing mothers and the sick . . . All available cabin accommodation was set aside for nursing and expectant mothers, for invalids and for women with young infants.' Others slept on mattresses on the troop decks and appointed, from among their own number, table attendants, sweepers and bathroom cleaners. There was a well-organised ship's hospital, which benefited from the services of 36 volunteers from among the evacuees, all with some previous hospital experience.

The Canadian Pacific ships undertook a long sea-voyage back to England, via Colombo, Durban and Capetown. Surgeon-Commander Goodfellow estimated that with the two American ships, they had taken five or six thousand evacuees out of Singapore. The *Empress of Japan* alone carried 1221 evacuees, of whom 222 disembarked at Colombo, where *Wakefield* and *West Point* were reported about the same time. At Colombo, the passengers learned of the fall of Singapore, where so many of them had left husbands and friends. Despite all they had seen before they left, the news still came as a great shock to them. They took it in very quietly, each with her own feelings about the past and each with her own problems to face in the future. Day-to-day, there were many young children on the ships, needing attention.

The *Empress of Japan* and the *Duchess of Bedford* kept much the same course, but sailed independently as they headed from Colombo for the Cape. At the South African ports of Durban and Capetown, a large number of the evacuees from Singapore left the *Empress* and some RAF and navy men were picked up. These servicemen joined fully into the spirit on board the evacuee ship by organising deck games and PE classes and entertaining the children. Members of the ship's own company and the evacuees themselves provided variety concerts as they made for the cold and dangerous waters of the North Atlantic and the hidden danger from German U-boats. At last, and to great relief, they were through it all and docking in Liverpool on 17 March 1942.

The experience of those who sailed on the *Duchess of Bedford* was not markedly different. Some of the passengers remembered this ship, with a mixture of affection and wry humour, as 'the drunken Duchess'. Built for the North Atlantic run, the *Duchess* had, it seemed, rolled a lot in the long and varied conditions of a sea-journey from South-East Asia to South Africa and the United Kingdom. Doris Pelton recalled a welcome short spell ashore at Durban and the extreme kindness which the evacuees had received from the women's organisations in South Africa. As with the *Empress*, the ultimate destination of the ship was the port of Liverpool, safely reached in April 1942.

The story of the part played by the *Duchess of Bedford* in the evacuation of large numbers of women and children from Singapore was very fully related in the memoirs of Mrs Barbara Parnell, who was working in the Malayan Auxiliary Medical Service and living in Ipoh when the Japanese army began its advance down the Malay Peninsula. Her husband was a captain in the Royal Signals in the Volunteers and she was to see him only briefly again before she left Singapore. He stayed, to become a prisoner-of-war in Changi, and then in Thailand, where he remained until the end of the war.

Barbara Parnell was ordered south from Ipoh during December 1941. She had little more than an hour's notice to leave and travelled by car with friends to Kuala Lumpur. Like so many other British expatriate women, she had to leave her home with all its contents, but she hoped her husband might still manage to have a trunk and chest, which she had packed, sent on by train. These did arrive for her in Singapore when she had continued south from Kuala Lumpur, having stayed with friends there in the meanwhile. A box which she had filled with family treasures remained under the stairs where it had been hidden and was not seen again. She arrived in Singapore in a train that had suffered from bomb blast at Ipoh station; all its windows had been blown out; at 3 a.m. she set about trying to contact friends there with whom she might stay. Singapore had not as yet suffered much from bombing attacks and there was some surprise at the arrival of civilian refugees from Ipoh and other 'up-country' places; Mrs. Parnell recalled that she 'managed to convince them that there was a war on'.

She reported for medical work and was sent to Raffles College, which was being used as a hospital for wounded Royal Navy men from the *Prince of Wales* and the *Repulse*. Women and children were leaving by ship for Australia, but Barbara Parnell had no wish to take that route. She wanted to stay in Singapore, 'hoping that things would improve'. Her two children were in Prestatyn, North Wales, with her husband's mother and sister and, if she moved anywhere, she was naturally anxious to rejoin them. She knew little or nothing about her husband's movements, but he turned up with the husband of a friend of hers in Singapore, with a message that army wives and children were being evacuated and, if there was room, the wives of Volunteers could go too. By this time troops had largely withdrawn from the mainland and Singapore was also full of civilian refugees.

The two husbands went to the Passport Office, which had moved out of town, and returned at 3 a.m. with a slip of paper containing the names of their wives and 'D of B', 'C Deck', written below. The message was to be on board ship by 2 p.m. that day. It was, recalled Barbara Parnell, the most miserable night of her life. Later, they made for the docks, taking only what they could carry, but the men did manage to get the trunk down also, on a truck which took them all. There was turmoil at the banks, where women were trying to get money and, during all this, Japanese bombers came over in a wave of attacks that continued for two or three hours. An ammunition ship near to the *Duchess of Bedford*, was, apparently, hit and 'there were dead all over the place', Mrs Parnell and her friend found their allocated deck-space on board the *Duchess* and their truck driver arrived back with a mattress for each of them and some sheets, brought from where they had been staying, just as they were. The two husbands, due back in camp, said farewell to their wives, the start of a long parting.

Indian soldiers were still disembarking and there were women and children everywhere, few of them recognisable in this dramatic situation. The ship was said to be filthy, with bathrooms and toilets useless; everything and everywhere needed a drastic clean-up and the women set to work to do this. On board, as Barbara Parnell recalled, were 1000 women and 400 children. They had hoped to sail out in the dark, but were still there next morning, mercifully leaving before the next spate of bombing. Leaving just ahead of them was the *Empress of Japan*. No one would say where they were going. Both ships, in fact, were reported as having called at Tanjong Priok (outport of Batavia) and holes caused by bomb damage or shrapnel on the *Duchess* were repaired. A gun and a party of Marines were also mounted on the ship. There followed an unsuccessful air attack on the ship *en route* (as it turned out) for Colombo. Here, they put in for five days and were allowed ashore, but instructed to say nothing about the ship. On the ship's radio, they heard the news of the fall of Singapore.

From Colombo, the *Duchess* zig-zagged to Durban, crossing the equator, it was said, no less than eight times. There was another break on shore at Durban, where local people, as in Colombo, were very kind to the evacuees from Singapore. Some army and RAF personnel embarked here, the army insisting that the ship be fumigated first. The long sea-voyage continued via Capetown, now with a reduced passenger load as many women and children were left at Durban.

After Capetown, strict black-out precautions were observed and all had to remain dressed all the time because of possible danger from German submarines. There was one further call, at Freetown, Sierra Leone, but no going ashore. Then it was the last anxious run to the United Kingdom, with arrival at Liverpool in April 1942. For the last two days at sea the passengers were heartened by the appearance of a British naval escort. But an overwhelming sense of gratitude was also felt to the captain of the *Duchess of Bedford* who had brought them so far and so safely under his own leadership.

About a week after the departure of the four big ships at the end of January 1942, another group of ships left Singapore just as Japanese troops were making their last preparations for a landing on the island. This included the Free French ship, *Felix Roussel*, and the *Devonshire*, both of which had only come into port the previous day. Between them, these two ships took out 2400 women and children, many of whom had either held back until this stage or simply been unable to get a passage earlier. A third vessel, *City of Canterbury*, carried 1700 RAF men, bound for Java; all were escorted through the Sunda Strait by HMAS *Hobart* and HMS *Electric*. In retrospect, with little more than a week left before Singapore would be surrendered to the Japanese, it was late for big merchant ships to be still seen in the docks there. Of the three further ships of 10 000 tons or more which still appeared there before fighting ceased, only one escaped.

On the *Felix Roussel* Marines Sergeant A. J. Willis had responsibility for looking after the welfare of the passengers, that is the evacuated women and children. He saw the task as one which required the exercise of clear authority, tempered by tact and impatience. He thought the scenes he witnessed in the Singapore dockyard 'might have come straight from Dante's *Inferno*', but, meanwhile, civilian sea-passages were still being booked and paid for, 'as for a P & O Cruise'. The ship's captain was an Irishman, MacBraine, the ship's officers were French and most of the crew were Lascars. On board, too, were 30 seamen and stokers from the *Empress of Asia* which had just been bombed and set on fire in the Outer Roads. There were eight civilian survivors from another sinking, all men from an American bank, and the rest of the passengers were women and children.

The *Felix Roussel* carried little for self-defence. A 4-inch gun was mounted astern and manned by another Marine, and there were to hand some American machine-guns, which no one seemed to know how to handle. Insecurity on the high seas was mitigated by the appearance of a British and Australian naval escort, but there were worried passengers who required attention. Some women had lost their children in the chaos which prevailed on the quayside; they were thought to be on another ship. Some children wandered round, looking for their mothers. All were in overcrowded conditions, living and sleeping just where they could. Water was severely rationed and no one knew how long the voyage would take or, perhaps except for the captain, where the intended destination lay. In fact, all arrived safely at Bombay, where Sergeant Willis was able to give up his special duty. Instead, he was to proceed by train and ferry to Ceylon, where he was required to report to the naval headquarters in Colombo!

The *Empire Star* had been part of the January convoy from Bombay to Singapore. This ship was owned by the Blue Star Line and in normal times served as a refrigerated cargo vessel between the United Kingdom and Australia and New Zealand. Although the ship displaced more than 11 000 tons, its passenger accommodation was very limited. It sailed from Singapore, making for Batavia, in the early hours of 12 February 1942, carrying RAF equipment and stores and a large passenger load. The ship's captain, Selwyn N. Capon, reported later that he had more than 2000 people on board, mostly naval, military and RAF personnel, but including at least 160 women and 35 children, some of the women being nurses from the 10th and 13th Australian General Hospitals. Least welcome was a party of drunken and undisciplined soldiers which had forced its way on to the ship shortly before departure. Two naval ships, *Durban* and *Kedah*, the latter in use as an auxiliary naval vessel, provided an escort to the *Empire Star* and to *Gorgon*, a Blue Funnel Line ship which was also carrying evacuees away from Singapore.

Shortly before 9 a.m. next morning, when the convoy was about to clear the Durian Strait, six Japanese dive-bombers attacked the *Empire Star*. Naval guns and machine-guns manned by RAF men made a quick response and one of the attacking planes crashed into the sea, while another was observed to be hit. But the *Empire Star* had sustained three direct hits, which killed 14 people and severely wounded 17 others, including two of the ship's crew; the ship was also badly damaged and set on fire in three places. Medical officers from the RAF tended the wounded and a fire-fighting squad, under the chief officer, tackled and extinguished the fires. In the words of a later report, this was 'a dangerous and difficult job in a ship thronged with people'.

Following the dive-bombing came twin-engined heavy bombers, with high-level attacks from 7000–10 000 feet. Planes engaged in this action came and went in relays over a period of four hours. A large number of bombs was dropped, many falling very close to the ship and one demolishing a lifeboat. By taking violent evasive action the captain kept his ship afloat and his passengers safe from further casualties. He and several members of his crew were later decorated for their courage, skill and quick action. When the grateful passengers reached Batavia, they disembarked until essential repairs were carried out and then some of them, at least, were taken on board again as the *Empire Star* left in a small convoy, making westwards at night through the Sunda Strait, escorted by HMS *Exeter*.

As appears later, Dutch ships were very prominent in a second stage of the Singapore evacuation, especially from Java and Sumatra. Among the Dutch vessels which successfully crossed the ocean westwards was *Plancius*, an inter-island passenger coaster of 5900 tons. This ship was built to accommodate 200–250 passengers in normal times, a small number by the standards of the big 17 000 ton Canadian Pacific liners, but big enough, in times that were far from normal, to contribute significantly to the movement of evacuees from

Batavia. As large numbers from Singapore arrived at the Dutch port, *Plancius* took on a new role, that of a kind of floating hotel, housing civilians who waited for ships bound for India or Australia. A small group of British naval officers, also waiting for trans-shipment pressed the Dutch captain to allow them to help sail the ship across the Indian Ocean, a proposal to which he finally consented. They left Batavia with 1000 passengers, every inch of deck-space taken and the holds full of people. Unescorted, *Plancius* progressed through the Strait of Sunda in thick fog and then headed well south before making westwards to Ceylon. All arrived safely at Colombo on 22 February. It had been a very fortunate voyage for what had become, in effect, a large evacuee ship, but one in which the navigation skills of British naval officers had played an important part.

In the late days of the Japanese war, two other big ships operated in and out of the region to the south of Singapore. The Dutch liner, *Zaandam*, lay at Tjiliatjap in southern Java when the Allied HQ in Java was breaking up and the defence of the island was passing to Dutch control. With a top speed of 21 knots, *Zaandam* was well placed and equipped to take remnants of military and RAF units, together with Naval Reservists not required on fighting ships, to Australia. It was often very much a matter of chance what categories of evacuee were picked up and at what port. Among those who boarded *Zaandam* were Peter Cardew, Public Works engineer from Malaya and, very recently, a Naval Reservist, and 'Paddy' Martin, peace-time planter in Johore and, recently, officer in the Johore Special Police and army liaison officer operating in and near the Johore Strait (see Chapter 4).

The Dutch liner stopped a short distance out of port to pick up survivors from the *City of Manchester* who were drifting in a lifeboat. The *City of Manchester*, a modern refrigerated cargo-liner of some 9000 tons, was apparently heading for Tjiliatjap with stores when attacked by the Japanese navy with torpedoes and shells. *Zaandam* picked up the occupants of the lifeboat, but two crew members were later reported to be missing. The Dutch ship then headed, at speed, well south on a zig-zag route, to Fremantle where it arrived without further incident.

About a week earlier, the Australian – Orient liner *Orcades* had sailed westwards from Batavia on the north coast of Java, certainly at that stage making a late escape and following the example set by *Plancius*. There was a mixed passenger list of evacuees, some of them having come out from Singapore on what was sometimes referred to

later as the '*Empire Star* convoy'. Among the passengers was Mrs
Muriel Reilly, formerly a cypher officer to the Governor of Singapore. She had left Singapore on the *Kedah*, a small coastal vessel,
crammed with 750 passengers, many of them RAF men making for
Java. Captain Sinclair, an ex-Singapore Harbour pilot, handled
Kedah with great skill, evading numerous attacks from Japanese
aircraft, and landed his passengers safely in Batavia. Here, Muriel
Reilly transferred to *Orcades*, a great contrast in size from her recent
rescue vessel, which she had known in better times on coastal
journeys from Singapore. No one could ever be sure what lay ahead
but many passengers on *Orcades* felt they might be with the ship on a
long voyage, possibly to the United Kingdom. At Colombo, however, all were ordered to disembark so that the ship could be further
employed in transporting Australian troops from the North African
front back to the defence of their own homeland.

Exceptionally, Mrs Reilly, who had made a very late and hasty
departure from Singapore, was allowed to stay on the *Orcades* as she
had no money with her and very few small possessions. In these
circumstances, she eventually reached Australia, having travelled via
Java and Ceylon.

The achievement of big ships in the business of evacuating both
military and civilian personnel from war zones in Singapore and
Indonesia (to use a later name) was remarkable, especially for the
number of women and children who were brought out in this way.
Their success depended heavily on the navigational skills of their
captains and other officers, and on the considerable measure of
boldness and initiative so often shown in the most perilous of circumstances. There were indeed casualties in these operations, but they
were mercifully small in relation to the number of big ships at risk
and the large passenger loads which they carried. Many of the people
transported safely from the bombing and shelling, and the fierce fires
in the Singapore docks, were to remember with affection for the rest
of their lives the name of the big ship which they had boarded there.
In similar circumstances, this was true also of a multiplicity of smaller
shipping and boats of all kinds which assisted in a late evacuation
effort from Singapore. But by this time the dangers were even greater
and the casualties in terms of boats and human lives rose accordingly.

In the overall course of the Second World War, both naval and merchant ships survived one crisis only to meet another one sooner or later. *Felix Roussel* survived the war and was prominent among the ships which brought back to England liberated prisoners-of-war from the Far East when the Japanese war was finally over. Some of the other ships mentioned here had met with disaster.

In September 1942, *Wakefield*, then in use as a naval transport, caught fire at sea and was, reportedly, towed into 'an Atlantic port', and described as 'nothing but a charred hulk'. On 7 November 1942, *Zaandam* was torpedoed and sunk off the east coast of the USA. Shortly before this, *Orcades* had been sunk by a German submarine operating in the South Atlantic; after a long ordeal in two lifeboats, some survivors were picked up by other ships in separate Atlantic locations.

The *Empire Star*, which had battled its way from Singapore to Java with large numbers of evacuees, was another casualty of war. Sailing from Liverpool in October 1942, and still under the command of Captain Capon the *Empire Star*, regarded as a fast ship, was routed independently and without escort, westwards, well out into the Atlantic. Apart from the ship's company, the vessel carried 19 passengers and a mixed cargo, which included aircraft and ammunition. It was not the first time the *Empire Star* had served as a military supply ship, but it was the last. On 23 October, the crew knew they were in mid-Atlantic, about 570 miles north of the Azores, and steaming south at 14 knots. This was their location when a torpedo struck, exploding on the starboard side amidships. One of the four lifeboats was destroyed by the explosion and, as the ship listed heavily to starboard, the captain gave the order to abandon ship. The engine-room flooded quickly and further torpedoes sank the ship while survivors were lying off in the three lifeboats, In a heavy sea, and with a gale blowing, the boats were separated during the night. Later, other ships located two of the lifeboats and their occupants; the third lifeboat was never seen again. It had held Captain Capon and 38 other people from the stricken ship.

There was another kind of evacuation, involving ocean-going shipping from Singapore. Miss Norah Inge was a teacher at a long-established mission school in central Singapore (Church of England

Zenana Missionary Society) when she was called upon by the Deputy Inspector-General of Police to help look after Japanese women and children who were being rounded up for internment purposes following the Japanese invasion of Malaya. The chosen location was the Indian immigration centre on St John's Island, off Singapore; here, by mid-January 1942, the numbers of Japanese women and children, formerly residents of Malaya and Singapore, had risen to about 1000. By this time, Kuala Lumpur was in Japanese hands and the battle for the Malay Peninsula was about to be fought out in the south, eventually on the island of Singapore itself. The Japanese internees had to be moved from St John's Island.

Miss Inge accompanied the internees on board a British India steamer which came to pick them up at the island and made for the open sea. British and Allied refugees were accommodated on the upper decks of the ship while the Japanese were in the holds for most of the time. Miss Inge's location lay uncomfortably between the internees in her charge and the mainly European women travelling 'above' on the same ship. They steamed south and west into the Indian Ocean, not to Colombo or Bombay, but to Calcutta. There appears to have been no major incident on this voyage, and from Calcutta the Japanese internees were taken by train westwards across Indian to Delhi. From here, they reached the vicinity of the Old Delhi Fort, where a special camp was set up for them. It was to be Norah Inge's home also until she and the internees all moved in 1943, to an oasis village in the Rajputana desert until after the end of the war. When the women and children arrived at this camp, a large number of Japanese men from Malaya and Singapore were already there. The story of their journey was outlined in a diary kept by K. Fukuda, one of their number, until July 1942 when it was confiscated by the camp authorities.

Japanese men resident in Singapore and Malaya were arrested from as early as 8 December and, within a few days, they were being transported to camp sites at Port Swettenham on the west coast of Malaya. The speed of the Japanese military advance down the peninsula cast serious doubts on the security of the Port Swettenham location and, before the end of December 1942, large groups of Japanese men were being brought back to Singapore. Some stayed for a short time in Outram Road prison, but soon all were apparently gathered in Changi gaol, a curious prologue to what would happen later, when British civilian internees would be crowded into that building. The Japanese were not there for long. On 7 January 1942, they were taken by trucks to Seletar on the north side of Singapore Island and shipped from there by steamer to what was for them an unknown destination. More than 1000 Japanese men were carried on the same ship as K. Fukuda. After passing through the Straits of Bangka and Sunda, they headed north-west through the Indian Ocean and arrived at the port of Bombay on 18 January.

In Bombay, the Japanese male internees were provided with warm clothing before being sent by train inland, reaching Delhi on 24 January. A further party of 660 Japanese men who had come from the opposite direction, by ship from Singapore to Calcutta and by train subsequently to Delhi, had just arrived there. The women and children were there the next day. With remarkable precision, some 2700 Japanese nationals had been transferred from Malaya and Singapore to arrive, at virtually the same time, in north central India at Delhi. Unlike the British internees under Japanese control later, where Japanese families were re-united they were allowed to live together.

Further small numbers of Japanese nationals brought the total at Delhi to about 2800, two-thirds of them men. The mass movement of Japanese civilians to India was unpublicised, for obvious reasons, at the time and seems to have had little historical notice since. It was achieved from Singapore while there was still a little time, and perhaps shipping, to spare. But not much. In less than a week after the Japanese internees were settled at Delhi, explosive charges were breaching the causeway between Johore and Singapore. The short final stage of the war in Malaya had arrived.

3 Java Routes

There was no long-term, or even medium-term, plan to evacuate British civilians or troops from Singapore in the event of a military defeat. The speed of the Japanese advance down the Malay Peninsula and the subsequent invasion of Singapore ensured that, at best, only hastily improvised plans could emerge to help people leave the island . These plans, at a late stage, constituted the 'official' evacuation and, outside of this, individuals and groups, both from the services and from civilian life, made their own attempts to escape capture, especially towards the end of resistance on the island.

After the large troop carriers taking away women and children had departed at the end of January and the Japanese had established a firm foothold on Singapore, planning began to focus on the evacuation of certain categories of both services people and civilians to Java on coastal-type vessels which would thread a route through the maze of islands to the south of Singapore, making for the Dutch capital at Batavia (Jakarta) and its outport, Tanjong Priok. Java was seen as the obvious fall-back area in the event of disaster at Singapore. It was the heartland of the Netherlands East Indies and the centre for the recently established American, British, Dutch Area Command (ABDA). If Singapore fell, Java, reinforced from outside, might still fill the role of stemming the Japanese advance and turning the tide of the war in the region.

A Dutch vessel, the *Rochuissen*, left Singapore for Java on 1 February 1942. Normally a cattle boat without passenger accommodation, the *Rochuissen* carried 200 passengers on this voyage, among them 50 members of the Malayan Broadcasting Corporation, now under orders to establish a station in Java, away from the bombing and shelling of Singapore. It was a very uncomfortable passage and the *Rochuissen* was bombed shortly after leaving Singapore, but not hit. The ship arrived at Tanjong Priok safely, four days after departure from Singapore.

Among the Broadcasting Corporation party was Enid Innes Ker, who had first arrived in Singapore in 1935 and subsequently married 'Tam', who was engaged in banking and other commercial activities there. When the *Rochuissen* sailed, Enid had her mother with her, but Tam was in the Straits Settlements Volunteers, manning a machine-gun post 'somewhere along the coast'. Husband and wife

34

did not meet again for more than three and a half years. Before the war, they had spent a short time in Penang and in Port Dickson but were back in Singapore in 1941 and it was here that Enid had joined the staff of the Malayan Broadcasting Corporation. She had started in an office at the top of Union Building, overlooking Collyer Quay; a humbler setting for the broadcasting station was to be sought in Java.

A makeshift radio station was set up and the MBC continued to operate from Java, but only for two weeks. With the surrender of Singapore, there proved to be little or no immediate purpose for a Malayan broadcasting unit in Java and, on 16 February, Mrs Innes Ker and a small party, including her mother, travelled by train from Batavia to Tjiliatjap on the south coast of the island. It was a long, hot journey through tropical mountain scenery and at the end of it there was another ship, the *Jagersfontein*, to carry evacuees to Australia. This latter ship left on 21 February and arrived in Melbourne ten days later. Subsequently, there was a train journey to Sydney. The sea voyage had been 'tedious, but not eventful' and this party had been among the more fortunate ones who avoided an encounter with the Japanese navy. Eventually, Mrs Innes Ker was to arrive in Scotland after sailing round the world, via New Zealand, the Panama Canal and the Atlantic! Her husband had, meanwhile, become a prisoner-of-war in Changi and, later, on the Burma – Siam railway.

———

Mrs Kathleen Stapledon was working as a clerk with the RAF in Singapore, where her husband was a naval architect. On 29 January, all servicemen's wives were told to leave Singapore and she was offered a passage out by ship. As she had no children, however, she chose to stay where she was, carrying on with her job. On 10 February, her husband phoned her to say that he thought the last passenger ship was about to leave the island and she should go with it. He had, in fact, already signed her on as a stewardess to ensure her passage. The ship was the Blue Funnel Line SS *Gorgon* (3533 tons), a mixed passenger-cargo vessel which could normally take up to 80 passengers. As the ship left for Batavia on 11 February, with Mrs Stapledon in her new role on board, it carried no less than 380 people, among them parties of 16 British and 32 Australian troops who had come out in a launch and small sampans, partly demanding, partly pleading to be taken on board. Alongside was another passenger ship and there were two escorting vessels. As they sailed south many other small ships stayed close to the *Gorgon*, heading in the same direction. During the passage of the Bangka Strait, the *Gorgon* and other vessels were bombed and machine-gunned by a flight of 27 Japanese planes. The ship nearest to the *Gorgon* received a direct hit but was able to continue; the *Gorgon* had several near-misses during heavy attacks on 12 February from both high-level and dive-bombing. Captain Marriott later thought that only the extreme manoeuvrability of the ship had saved her.

Most vessels on this route made for Tanjong Priok, the outport of Batavia, but *Gorgon* disembarked the military personnel and went straight ahead for Australia, arriving safely at Fremantle. The *Darvel*, under Captain Hugh Jones, also reached Australia, but was less fortunate *en route*. Heavily bombed and machine-gunned in the Bangka Strait, *Darvel* suffered serious damage. The 'near misses', in Captain Jones's words, 'nearly crippled us'. There were casualties, too, among the troops on board. Three were killed and buried at sea and 49 were injured. In Tanjong Priok, the ship needed emergency repairs – there were 370 holes to be blocked on the starboard side alone. There was a serious question as to whether the ship was seaworthy, but the captain obtained permission to leave on 27 February. In a severe storm and rough sea, some 120 miles from the coast of Western Australia, the plugged holes gave way and it became difficult to keep out the sea and hold the vessel in control. But they reached Fremantle in the end and the grateful passengers disembarked, to look for assistance on their own account in Australia.

The *Jalna Krishna* and the *Kedah* also sailed from Singapore only two or three days before the surrender. The *Jalna* had a heavy passenger load ('we were packed like sardines') and was repeatedly dive-bombed by Japanese aircraft during the first two days out of port. By skill and good fortune, the ship escaped a direct hit and arrived at Tanjong Priok, for Batavia, on 14 February. Among the disembarking passengers was Mrs Frances Clarke, who had worked as an auxiliary hospital nurse, first in Malacca, then in Singapore. At her husband's request she had left Singapore at a late stage (their children having been evacuated a little earlier) and she had little with her

but the clothes she wore. With other evacuees, she stayed for a short
time on board SS *Plancius*, which was being used to accommodate
them. Then they left on a hazardous journey through the Sunda
Strait into the Indian Ocean and on to Colombo. They were uncomfortable, on a crowded ship with little food and less water, but were
fortunate in avoiding air and submarine attack; they arrived in
Colombo on 27 February.

The *Kedah* was known to Mrs Muriel Reilly as a little coastal ship
on which she and her husband had often sailed to attend race
meetings in Pahang. When the *Kedah* left Singapore in the grim days
shortly before the surrender it carried a heavy passenger load of
civilian and RAF servicemen *en route* to Batavia. Repeatedly, the
little ship was dive-bombed by Japanese aircraft; repeatedly, the
captain's skill in manoeuvring saved the ship and everyone on board.
Many of the RAF played their part by lying on the deck and firing off
any weapon they had to hand as the hostile planes came in. They
helped to impede the low-level attacks.

Mrs Reilly had worked in the cipher office at government headquarters in Singapore and was one of the late evacuees, leaving with
scarcely any effects, and no money. Fortunately, she was helped by a
Dutch hotelier to stay for a few days in Batavia and then to join a
large liner, the *Orcades*, which took a further shipload of refugees
safely from Java to Colombo, arriving there at the end of February.
While thankful to be on such a large ship, Mrs Reilly thought the
smallness of the *Kedah* had been a real asset in her escape from the
Japanese bombs *en route* to Java.

Muriel Reilly's travels were not at an end in Colombo, for the
Orcades was promptly required to take Australian troops back to
defend their homeland; these were units which had been recalled
from North Africa at the urgent insistence of the Australian government. The ship's captain granted Mrs Reilly's request to stay on
board and sail to Australia, where she was destined to spend the rest
of the war years (see Chapter 2).

Chris Noble was an Australian who worked in the Malayan Survey
Department in Kuala Lumpur and happened to be on leave with his
wife and children in Tasmania when the Japanese invaded Malaya.
He was almost due back in Malaya, but it looked doubtful at first

whether he would be able to secure any kind of passage. Considering it his duty, however, to return if at all possible, he made his way to Sydney and, by securing a priority air booking, reached Singapore on 14 December. Two days later, he was back at work in his old department in Kuala Lumpur.

After less than a month, and just ahead of the Japanese advance on Kuala Lumpur, Mr Noble and his colleagues were packing up materials and stores and moving south to Singapore, where some were billeted in the Tanglin ballroom. Three or four weeks later, they were packing up again, this time for a move to Java. The departmental head told his staff that 'nothing but a miracle' could save Singapore and that married men should get their wives away on the first possible ship. Stocks of maps which could not be moved were to be burned at once and orders were given to damage map-printing machinery now likely to fall into Japanese hands.

Hurriedly, the wives of Survey staff who were still in Singapore were summoned to board the *Ipoh*, an old Straits steamer. Some stores and equipment had already gone forward on the Java route and as the unit in Singapore was being disbanded, some of the men also left with the *Ipoh*. Before the ship sailed, 300 RAF men embarked and, again, there was a bad case of overcrowding. Normally the *Ipoh* took only 30 passengers and now the ship had a serious 'list' even before attracting the attention of Japanese aircraft.

Like most other ships leaving Singapore around that date (11 February), the *Ipoh* faced heavy enemy air attacks in the Bangka Strait. The RAF mounted a dozen machine guns on deck and used these to some effect in limiting low-level attacks. The ship's captain, like many others caught in the same situation, performed wonders in creating a zig-zag pattern to avoid the bombs and there was no direct hit on the *Ipoh*, though much incidental damage arose from near misses and shrapnel. Overloaded and listing badly, the *Ipoh* limped into the outport for Batavia on 14 February, the day before the fall of Singapore.

During the next few days a convoy of some ten small ships was assembled at Batavia for passage to Australia. Most of these vessels fell far short of standards which could be expected from ocean-going craft, but it was no time for debating niceties of this kind. Chris Noble sailed on the *Whang Pu*, a former Chinese river-boat of low draught. Loaded on this and other vessels sailing at the same time were 71 crates of Malayan Survey Department material, including a large number of glass plates which needed careful packing and handling. British and Dutch destroyers, most of which were sunk later, escorted the convoy and the Sunda Strait was negotiated at night. It was no small test of courage and endurance for slow-moving ships to be heading through Sunda at this time, as a submarine threat added to the other dangers; a torpedo which narrowly missed the *Whang Pu* provided a chilling reminder. However, Mr Noble recorded his safe arrival off Fremantle on 28 February and his landing there two days later. It was little more than six weeks since he had left Australia and hastened back to Malaya from leave.

The staff of the Survey Department did not all escape from Singapore in this manner. Some were still on the island and were interned in Changi, others were among those shipwrecked. More by chance than anything other members of institutional groupings also reflected this varied range of experiences in the dramatic circumstances of the loss of Singapore.

The sea-voyage from Singapore to Java comprised about 600 miles of island-dotted seaways, a distance which was lengthened when ships took evasive action to avoid air attacks. The time for the journey was also prolonged when shelter was sought at island inlets on the way. Yet, for a number of reasons, Batavia and its outport, Tanjong Priok, was the main objective for evacuee vessels leaving Singapore in the last week of the fighting there. Batavia was a large city and port area and benefited from the resources of a well-populated hinterland. From Batavia, as was the case in Singapore, there were many established shipping routes. As the earlier capital and main government centre of the Netherlands East Indies, Batavia had been developed over three centuries and more, whereas, by comparison, most of the east coast of Sumatra, though nearer to Singapore, was relatively undeveloped and had no major port over a long stretch of swampy coastline.

In southern Sumatra there was an important river port at Palembang and south from there again there was a rail connection to Oosthaven (Teluk Betung), which looked out upon the Sunda Strait and had a ferry service to Java. Only those who arrived from Singapore early, however, were normally able to benefit from the Palembang – Oosthaven route. While a stream of vessels was at sea from Singapore, a Japanese naval task-force established a base at Muntok on the north of the island of Banka, and Japanese paratroops landed in the Palembang area. By mid-February, the direct sea-route to Java via the Bangka Strait was being effectively sealed off by the Japanese, but this news reached many rescue vessels too late. In a critical period of two or three days, shipping from Singapore was bombed, shelled, beached and captured, much of this taking place in the Bangka Strait. Only when the true position was realised did the advice circulate, through Dutch authorities, that the river estuaries of eastern central Sumatra offered an alternative and safer route. It was a route without major reception ports and its success would depend on a crossing of the island of Sumatra to a more distant port on the west side with access to the Indian Ocean.

Few evacuees from Singapore reached Palembang in safety, but among those who did were some officials of the Singapore Harbour Board. The first of three such groups, this party left Singapore on the *Bagan* on 11 February, accompanied by a number of women and children. They reached Palembang only hours ahead of the Japanese landings there and continued by rail to Oosthaven and by sea to Batavia, where they arrived on the 14th, still with a chance of finding a ship to Ceylon or Australia. Another ship, *Klias*, reportedly left Singapore on 11 February and reached the Palembang (Moesi) River. There it was scuttled to avoid capture, but the ship's company was still able to continue to Batavia by train and ferry. Within about 24 hours of these journeys, Japanese troops were in control of the Palembang area and the Japanese navy was patrolling the Bangka Strait.

Already, evacuee ships had been bombed and sunk at no great distance south of Singapore. Among these were the *Kuala* and the *Tun Kuang* (*Tien Kwang*), both sunk off the small island of Pom Pong, but it was in the Bangka region where the casualties were to be greatest. Most of the 40 or so rescue vessels which left Singapore only to be destroyed or captured by the Japanese met their fate in the Bangka Strait. As Rohan Rivett, of the Malayan Broadcasting Corporation, was to put it, retrospectively, 'most of the shipping that lay around us that afternoon [Singapore, 11 February] was at the bottom of the ocean in and around the Bangka Strait within the next seven days'.

In the course of three or four mid-February days in 1942, some 23 rescue ships from Singapore were sunk or captured in or near the Bangka Strait. Many of the ships were carrying the wives and children of regular servicemen and of British civilian expatriates who had been working in Malaya. In the circumstances of the late evacuation from Singapore, groups of servicemen were often mixed with civilians on the same boat. In the tropical daylight, ships out on the open sea were mercilessly exposed to air attack, while at night, in the Bangka Strait, several ships sailed into the near range of a Japanese naval squadron, came under searchlights and were shelled, sunk or captured. The more fortunate ones were directed into Muntok harbour, on the north side of Bangka, or were beached nearby.

The *Chiang Bee* left Singapore with a total complement of about 300 evacuees. Lifeboats were lowered when the ship was halted by the Japanese navy but it was thought there were still about 100 people on board when the ship was shelled. An explosion appeared to light the *Chiang Bee* from stem to stern and the vessel sank rapidly. Although some survivors were picked up, only to be captured subsequently by the Japanese, as many as 200 lives were probably lost in one way or another in this one incident.

The *Vyner Brooke* also left Singapore in this period (12 February) with 200 or more evacuees, mainly civilians and army nurses. They were bombed and sunk off the north end of the Bangka Strait and those who survived landed on Bangka from boats and rafts or by swimming or floating in the water. Here again, casualties were high, about half the total number of passengers on board. Loss of life at sea was not the end of the tragedy in this case, for parties of Japanese troops rounded up some of the shipwrecked men on the island and bayoneted them and many women were machine-gunned in the shallow water. Two men and one woman (an Australian nurse) survived this ordeal by good fortune, the nurse with a bullet hole in her side, to be living witnesses of the atrocity.

Another ship, the *Mata Hari*, sailing about the same time, survived bombing attacks on the Java route only to be captured by the Japanese navy in the Bangka Strait and directed into Muntok. This coastal cargo ship, taken over by the Admiralty just before the war, was carrying a large number of passengers but, mercifully, the passengers and crew were landed without serious casualties. They joined ship-wrecked groups from the *Vyner Brooke* and other vessels in miserably squalid surroundings on Bangka. It was the beginning of a period of three and a half years' internment in camps in Bangka and Sumatra; many died before the war was over.

The evacuee ships on the Java route had sailed without knowledge of what lay ahead of them. The *Kuala* alone carried about 500 passengers, more than half of whom were civilians. A further rescue

attempt from Pom Pong by the *Tanjong Pinang*, which called in
response to distress signals, was an even worse disaster. The ship was
sunk, almost without trace, with the loss of virtually 180 women and
children and 20 wounded, all priority evacuees. The escape of a
nursing sister, Margot Turner, from this latter shipwreck was a story
of outstanding physical and moral courage. Only after much tragedy
and loss of life did a message begin to circulate round the islands still
free of the Japanese that Java was no longer the place to be making
for; the shorter run to eastern Sumatra now became the preferred
route.

An account left by Major J. W. P. Marsh, officer-in-charge of Base
Ordnance Workshops (MT) in Singapore, illustrates the experience
of a small, selected army group chosen for evacuation from Singapore. He was in charge of a party of 28 men instructed to board the
Poelau Soegi, a motor boat of 150 tons, on the evening of Friday 13
February 1942. They were said to be making for Java and at daylight
next morning they could see many islands and numerous ships of all
kinds and sizes. Soon, Japanese bombers were attacking other small
craft and the captain of the *Poelau Soegi* was estimating that, taking
shelter where they could, it might take them a week to reach Java.

In the distance, they sighted a naval squadron, which, to their great
consternation, turned out to be Japanese. They quickly altered
course in an attempt to get out of range, but, at this stage, the
Japanese appeared to take no notice of them. Major Marsh lay on the
deck most of the time, 'almost played out', suffering from stomach
trouble and general exhaustion; he may have lost count of time.
Suddenly, at night, he was aroused by a loud explosion and a flash of
light. A shell had hit the other side of the smokestack from where he
was lying. Almost at once, a blaze of light from two large searchlights
swept the motorboat and men were jumping into the water away
from the light. Marsh jumped too, as shelling continued and screams
rose from the water.

The Major had a lifebelt on and, though he felt too weak to swim,
he was able to float on his back and release his boots and socks. As
he drifted through the water he could see his late rescue vessel
blazing through the night. Two lighthouses could be seen ahead, but
at daylight he was still perhaps two or three miles from a shore and
feeling 'all in'. Then a large ship loomed up, the *Kwai Maru*, full of
Japanese troops. Major Marsh was lucky enough to be taken on
board and be seen by an English-speaking Japanese doctor. His feet
were badly cut and he was extremely tired. As he recovered a little,

he found that he had arrived at Muntok where he was to join other prisoners and internees. Two-thirds of the 70 or 80 men on board the *Poelau Soegi* lost their lives in the shelling and in the water.

There was one recorded attempt to escape from Bangka and Muntok. Rohan Rivett had left Singapore on 12 February on the *Siang Wo*, a Yangste river boat of 2500 tons, which he shared with about 230 other passengers. Before nightfall on the next day, they were bombed off Bangka; the boat, badly damaged, was run on to the island to save lives and beached there. Landing close to Muntok, it was quickly apparent to the stranded passengers that they would soon be prisoners of the Japanese. Rivett and six other men decided to make a bid for freedom by setting off on foot to cross the mountains on the island and meet the coast again further to the south-west, putting as great a distance as they could between themselves and the Japanese base at Muntok. Eventually. down the coast, they were able to secure a Malay boat and were joined by another group of men who had been operating separately, but with the same escape idea.

This combined party of refugees attempted to reach Java in the small boat and eventually succeeded in doing so. But time was not on their side. More than three weeks had passed since the *Siang Wo* had beached on Bangka and by now Japanese patrols were operating in western Java and intimidating any Javanese who might have given assistance to fugitives. It had been a very brave effort but it was all to end in capture by Japanese troops.

As the island of Java came under threat of Japanese attack, Batavia was declared an 'open city' and the one sizeable port left open on the island so far as escape movements were concerned lay in the south at Tjiliatjap. From Padang and its outport, Emmahaven, in western Sumatra (see Chapters 4 and 5), it was possible to despatch shipping to Tjiliatjap which could arrive there safely until about the end of February. The main danger area was the southern end of the Sunda Strait, which had to be crossed. As late as 24 February, the Dutch ship *Duijmeyer Van Twist* took 500 passengers from Padang to

Tjiliatjap; the ship had normal passenger accommodation for 28 people and no special food provisions. It was on this occasion carrying a cargo of tinned fish and rice, which became the staple diet of the servicemen, civilians and members of the Volunteer services who made this voyage. The Sunda Strait was crossed safely, but not without some anxiety, and at Tjiliatjap further arrangements were made. Naval officers and ratings joined the destroyer *Stronghold* and some reserve naval officers joined the sloop *Bernie*. The rest of the passengers of the *Van Twist* were directed to a modern Dutch liner, *Zaandam*, which left port quickly, picking up, on the second day out, 43 survivors in a lifeboat of the *City of Manchester*. The *Zaandam* could reach a speed of 21 knots and made for Australia on a zig-zag route, arriving safely at Fremantle on 7 March. The destroyer *Stronghold* was sunk two days after the rendezvous in Tjiliatjap.

Among those who landed from the *Van Twist* at Fremantle was 'Paddy' Martin, formerly manager of the Sungei Papan estate in Johore and latterly an intelligence and liaison officer with the British army in Johore and Singapore. He was aware of his good fortune in reaching Australia after an escape bid which had started in Johore three weeks earlier (see Chapter 4). He could not yet be aware that he would return to India, join the army and Force 136, and be taken back for special operations work in Japanese-occupied Malaya in September – October 1944. Here, tragically, he was ambushed and killed, paying the full military price for the freedom he had won by his escape from Singapore in 1942.

A hospital ship was stated to have left Batavia on a westward voyage as late as 23 February 1942, but it was torpedoed in the Indian Ocean; a tanker picked up survivors and landed them at Goa. By late February, however, Batavia was no longer the place to be looking for an evacuee ship; the main remaining outlet to the sea lay on the other side of the island of Java at Tjiliatjap, to which there were road and rail connections. Even here, time and opportunity were both limited. In a recently published account, Jane Tierney has told of missing a ship at Tjiliatjap and returning inland to seek shelter at a convent of Dutch nuns near Purbolingo. Japanese troops had arrived there in the meantime and she found herself a prisoner. She escaped, however, with just time to reach Tjiliatjap again and board an old ship taking out wounded RAF men. It was a risky voyage and they were soon bombed and machine-gunned, with the loss of five lives. The ship was also very slow and they were short of food and, in due course, of fuel. But they were fortunate enough to complete the run to Western Australia and freedom.

The members of the staff of the American Consulate in Singapore were evacuated on what was later described as on 'a ten-knot freighter' to Batavia at the end of January 1942. Among those on the move was Eileen Niven, American wife of a young British engineer in the Malayan Public Works Department. The American party made the crossing safely to Java, and Eileen, who had a clerical job with the Consulate, was first lodged in the splendid Hotel des Indes in Batavia, then attached to a military headquarters near Bandoeing. Here, within a week of Mrs Niven's arrival, the neighbouring airfield was heavily bombed and preparations were soon made for another move further south. At Tjiliatjap, she found herself with others waiting for a plane to Australia and, on 24 February, she flew to Broome, the nearest airfield in north-west Australia. It was another route out of Java and Dutch air pilots were flying it at mounting risk, as with everything else. In Australia, a flight inland was possible as far as Alice Springs, then, with a change of plane, Eileen Niven was conveyed to Sydney. However, there were neither the aircraft nor the previous patterns of air services in the region to facilitate any large-scale evacuation by air and this case, though not unique, must be seen as highly exceptional as a 'Java route'.

Equally exceptional, but in a very different way, was the experience of RAF Sergeant Charles McCormac. Heavily engaged in motor transport work, bringing refugees across the causeway from Johore to Singapore, he saw his wife leave Singapore at the last minute on the *Wakefield* at the end of January. Subsequently, he helped to man a road block on the Bukit Timor Road near Woodlands, and his published account described a dramatic encounter with a Japanese patrol, in which he shot three Japanese soldiers and was then taken prisoner and held in a very mixed camp of British, Australians and Asians, engaged on clearing and cleaning up work in the Singapore docks area. From this camp, at Pasir Pajang, McCormac and 16 others, the members of a working party, made a bold and determined attempt to escape; many of them, including McCormac himself, felt they had nothing to lose, as they lived in an atmosphere of interrogations, torture and executions.

Sergeant McCormac's escape from Singapore island was accomplished by means of a bold dash to the north coast to pick up boats near Kranji, as arranged for them by a Eurasian sympathiser. There were heavy casualties on the way and this stage of the escape plan ended with only four men drifting in one boat from the Johore Strait westwards into the open sea. They were short of food and even more desperately short of water. By an intervention which seems to have been little short of the miraculous, they were spotted and picked up from the sea by a seaplane of the Royal Netherlands Air Force and flown to Medan in Sumatra. From there they undertook a journey of 800 miles down the east coast of Sumatra, moving as best they could. A Chinese lorry driver eventually drove them to Palembang as they lay hidden under rubber sheets in his lorry. They used similar camouflage on a freight train from Palembang to Oosthaven, found a small boat to take them to an adjacent island and a larger boat from there to carry them across the Sunda Strait. By this time, the whole region through which they were passing was under Japanese control but they were helped and guided in Java by nationalist guerillas along jungle and coastal routes to Tjiliatjap and further east.

Eventually, they reached the hideout of an Australian liaison officer who arranged for them, by radio, to be flown out from the Java coast on a seaplane arriving at night from Broome. It was 16 September, seven months after the fall of Singapore and more than five months since the breakout from Pajang. Only McCormac and his closest companion, an Australian named Donaldson, had made it all the way. One member of the escape party died in Java from dysentery and general weakness; the remaining member chose to stay in Java.

Another RAF man, Corporal John Dodd, was evacuated with RAF groupings from Singapore to Batavia on the *Empire Star*. In the account of his experience written by Diana Norman, Corporal Dodd recalled that the ship carried more than 1200 passengers (2000 in the captain's account) while 16 would have been the limit under normal conditions. Armed Australian soldiers had rushed the gangplank to get on board, whereupon the ship's captain had ordered it to be raised to avoid further incidents of this kind. They were bombed *en route* to Java and there were casualties among the RAF. When they reached Batavia, the RAF personnel were dispersed to rest stations.

Before long, however, they were on the move again, this time southwards towards Tjiliatjap. John Dodd was reluctant to be re-grouped and leave Java and he also had a dental problem he was trying to have put right. In the end, he was on the road to Tjiliatjap, first by taxi, then by car. His companions were a Eurasian mother and daughter and an American air pilot. They found the approaches to Tjiliatjap blown up and there was no news of a ship. Heading further west, they reached Genteng in south-west Java and finally, Palaboehan Ratoe. After this, they went into hiding, not easily recognising who might help them and who would betray them. Eventually, they were captured by Japanese troops and Dodd was fiercely interrogated and tortured, but he managed to survive this period and imprisonment for the rest of the war.

The confusion in Java among the remnants of British and Allied soldiers and airmen who had been evacuated from Singapore was considerable. Whatever further defensive role was envisaged against the Japanese in Java, nothing happened on a large scale, and for several reasons. There was, first, a time-factor, as Japanese military movements seemed to follow so quickly one after another. There was an obvious lack of reinforcements or new resources, and a policy of designating the Batavia area and other towns 'open'. Lasting resistance, as in Malaya, was to be found in guerilla camps and this took time to organise and have much effect. The British and Allied military headquarters was withdrawing through Tjiliatjap, less than two months after it had been set up, at the time when there was still fighting in central Malaya. It is against this background that indivi-

dual British and Allied experiences in Java in late February 1942
need to be weighed.

A. G. Banfield had worked in Malaya for four years before the war
and was returning from leave in England in November 1941. Before
going on leave he had been in training with the Volunteers in Malaya
where he held the rank of sergeant-major. His return journey to
Malaya was a long one, from Liverpool, via Panama, the Pacific and
Australia. He disembarked in Java, eventually, too late to reach
Singapore before the Japanese. He was quickly assigned duties in his
role of sergeant-major and he found himself busy in transit camps for
British and Australian troops who had reached Java from Singapore.
Having come round much of the world only to approach Singapore
too late, he had only arrived just in time to spend two or three weeks
in Java! He sailed away from Tjiliatjap on 28 February, almost as late
as anyone and yet he arrived safely in India.

A very high price in human lives and misery, as well as in shipping of
many kinds, was paid on the sea-route between Singapore and Java
in the days close to the surrender of Singapore to the Japanese.
William McDougall, a former press correspondent in the Far East,
whose fate it was to be shipwrecked and then imprisoned in Palembang, estimated that 3000 lives were lost in and near the Bangka
Strait. The casualties were almost all on evacuee vessels, though at
least one act of great naval courage, the firing at close range of a
single gun at a Japanese naval vessel by the naval auxiliary HMS *Li
Wo*, was recorded. Among those who lost their lives when bound for
Java were many sailors who had survived the sinking of the *Prince of
Wales* in the South China Sea at the very beginning of the Malayan
Campaign. One party of these naval evacuees was among the 120
men on the *Li Wo*, which sank off Bangka with very few survivors.
   In retrospect, it is clear that the odds against successful escape
from Singapore to Java in February 1942, were much greater than
most of those who took part could have foreseen. Great dangers also
hung over sea routes from Java, whether to Sumatra or, more

distantly, to India or Australia. This is not to deny that, even with greater knowledge of what might lie ahead, many would still have faced the challenges willingly. There was no measure or rule, however, by which it could have been predicted who would cross the seas safely and who would perish. Some would die in a second shipwreck having survived a first one. Others would escape from a sinking ship, only to linger, and perhaps die, in squalid captivity. A few of those who ultimately escaped to freedom would be back in the Malayan area again later in the war, taking on a new challenge and new risks.

To those who left Singapore on or about the time of the British surrender, Java had, at best, offered temporary respite and the chance of a further sea-passage. Alternative sea-routes, really suited only to the small types of coastal and river shipping, were to focus on a central section of the eastern Sumatran coastline, which had wide river estuaries and rivers which could be navigated for quite long distances inland by shallow-draught vessels. What quickly became an orthodox escape route via Sumatra was a remarkable complex of river, road and rail journeys with a town and port facing the Indian Ocean at the end of it. It is time now to consider the experiences of some of those who travelled this way.

4 By Sea to Sumatra

Many small craft successfully carried people away from a stricken Singapore to the east coast of Sumatra. At its shortest, the distance to the central coastal area was little more than 40 miles but few, if any, managed a short crossing. Rapidly changing circumstances rather than original choice made the wide river mouths along the coast of eastern Sumatra the targets of late escape runs from Singapore. Routes were changed according to information received, anchorage and shelter were sought in small islands *en route*; some of these also served as staging points, allowing transfers between boats. Food and water supplies had to be procured frequently.

On the night of 13/14 February 1942, a company of military volunteers from the 18th Division was brought together in Singapore to form an official escape party. A larger and more ambitious plan foundered when sufficient launches or other vessels could no longer be found, but three boats were earmarked to take 100 officers and men; the rest of the troops were to return to their units or, with the dangers explained, attempt to leave the island by individual effort. It was the evening of 14 February and Singapore would be surrendered to the Japanese next day. A small group of nine men, mostly from the Northumberland Fusiliers, led by Major B. J. Leech, procured two boats near the docks and rowed away from the island just after midnight. At 3.30 a.m. they waded ashore on St John's Island. It was a modest start.

The escape plan at this stage was to proceed in a south-easterly direction as far as the island of Singkep, then along the coast of Sumatra to reach the island of Bangka, where they hoped to find a steamer passage to Batavia. The wind was from the north-east and they hoped 'to put up some sort of sail' on the 18-foot boat, which they now named *Pushme-Pullu*. After an overnight stay on St John's Island, they were joined by another soldier who had swum across from Blakang Mati island during the night. They then rowed across to the next island, where they made contact with a Colonel and eight men in a sailing junk. The Colonel agreed to take them in tow, one of the two original boats being abandoned as a result of this move.

Towing proved to be a slow and erratic business, so, after three or four hours, they cast off and began rowing again in a choppy sea. In the late afternoon they landed on a sandy beach on Pulau Samboe.

Throughout the day there had been 'an incessant rumble' from the direction of Singapore and several times formations of bombers had flown overhead, making towards Singapore. Thick, oily-grey smoke could be seen in the distance, but, gradually, noises faded and all was quiet. It was, approximately, the time of the cease-fire in Singapore.

Fortunately, the escape party included a fluent Malay speaker in J. R. Miller of the Federated Malay States Volunteers. On a reconnaissance to the neighbouring island of Blakang Padang, Miller was able to negotiate with the local Malays for two sails, a large one and a small one, and the accompanying equipment in the form of a ten-foot bamboo mast, wire stays, heavy ropes, additional wire and the like. A Malay boatman made and fitted everything on the spot, including a main halyard with block and tackle. An axe and cooking pot were added to the overall equipment and *Pushme-Pullu* left the island as a sailing boat, though a rather clumsy one, handled by a very amateur crew. A useful map of the whole area between Singapore and Sumatra was a further treasure picked up at Blakang Padang. By the end of that day (16 February), *Pushme-Pullu* had put in to the south side of Pulau Bojan and a steady wind on the next day helped them to reach Pulau Setoko, where the islanders were able to supply coconuts, fish, salt, rice, coffee and sugar.

A small sailing boat brought Wallace Little and Douglas Richardson to the same island. They were members of the Malayan Volunteers Forces, both with a substantial previous background in the Malayan Civil Service. They brought the alarming news that the Japanese were on the island of Bangka and, nearer still, had captured Tanjong Pinang, capital of the Rhio group of islands. In the event, the report about Tanjong Pinang was premature, but a Dutch evacuation was in progress there, as both escape parties agreed to head together in a south-westerly direction and a near route to the Sumatra coast. Corporal Sidey and Fusiler Bennett from Major Leech's boat joined Little and Richardson to spread the tasks more evenly. The intention now was to follow the line of the Sumatran coast, making rendezvous arrangements as they went along.

Another overnight island stop was made on 18/19 February and the island of Pulau Moro Besar was reached in the late afternoon of the 19th. A dinghy towing a yacht with a dozen officers and men on board was hailed and Major Leech's crew were rewarded with the information that there was a ration dump at the northern end of Moro Besar. This boat party was not without its problems as they often had long periods of hard rowing, Leech had a poisoned leg, many had cut feet and Miller was prone to bouts of malaria. They arranged with Little that his sailing boat would divert to investigate the ration dump and they would all meet again, further south, at the island of Doerei. This plan worked, except that the second boat had a particularly difficult time and arrived a day late. Major Leech's men, too, were very tired as they put into a small island, just south of Doerei. Here, a Chinese charcoal trader provided welcome hospitality.

The four men on the sailing boat duly found the ration dump and a message to say that escape parties should go up the Indragiri River to a place given as 'Prigi Raja'; this fitted well with the change of plan. The Malay-speaking Miller learned from islanders on Doerei that several parties of soldiers had passed that way in sailing boats and motorboats, while others had been sunk. Arrangements were now made for a Malay guide from the island to accompany everyone to the Sumatran coast. This assurance together with a welcome cooked meal raised spirits all round.

It was difficult to distinguish between news items and rumours; a story that the Japanese had occupied Setoko and were expected shortly at Moro Besar hastened the departure of Major Leech's now combined party from Doerei. They sailed in a Malay boat, at last, and with mixed feelings, leaving *Pushme-Pullu* behind. On a night sailing they reached Guntong, where they met 16 other officers and men, including the yacht party they had seen near Moro Besar. After eight days they had reached the swampy deltas of central eastern Sumatra and there was still much travelling ahead. A further river journey was followed by a night in a disused camp near Tanjong Lanjaut, where there was a junction between a jungle path and the river. There followed, early next morning, a trek of several hours along the jungle path, carrying all they had, then a river sampan again and, finally, the sampan was towed by motorboat from Chariah Manda to Tembilahan. At every stage there had to be negotiation and bargaining for boats and guides. Burned by the sun, drenched by tropical rain, bitten by mosquitoes and land crabs, the 12 men reached this last haven on 24 February. About 100 British troops from Singapore were already there and no boats were available.

On the positive side, villagers on the islands had been generous in providing food and water, and the one or two District Officers whom they had met had helped them on their way. On a beached Dutch oil tanker off Doerei they had found some old navigational charts, which, though out of date, gave them some idea of their situation in a confusing scene of islands, mangrove swamps, deltas, rivers and streams. By bearing south-west, more or less in line with the Sumatran coast, they had successfully avoided identification and attack by Japanese aircraft. They had often seen reconnaissance planes and bombers, sometimes very low, but they had been ignored. They could rightly feel that it was no small achievement to have reached Sumatra in their small boats.

William ('Paddy') Brereton Martin was the manager of Sungei Papan estate in south Johore when the Japanese advanced down the Peninsula. At the end of December 1941, he was enrolled as an officer in a newly created unit of Johore Special Police which was to provide guides and interpreters for the military and also carry out duties of food controlling and general policing. Working with him in the same role was his deputy manager from the estate, a man named Browning; between them they had to attempt to cover a large area to the east of the Johore river, eventually from Kota Tinggi southwards to Pengerang on the south coast. Their main links with the military related to a battalion stationed at Pengerang in Johore and to the military base at Changi on Singapore island. On making strong representations to Changi, they were provided with a wireless transmitting station at Papan and a naval patrol of three armed motor-sampans manned by British officers and Malay ratings.

On 27 January 1942, General Percival was recognising that the military situation in Johore was 'critical'. Two days earlier, Paddy Martin ensured that his wife and child sailed from Singapore for India and then he was busy developing what was to be an early warning system against possible Japanese landings on the east coast of Johore. The land lines which he ordered from Singapore never reached him, but events, in any case, were moving quickly to a crisis. By 30 January, it was being reported that Japanese patrols had reached Kota Tinggi and both the Papan wireless station and the naval motor-sampans were withdrawn to Singapore. The Papan estate was the last one to be working under British management as Japanese advance units reached southern Johore, and the battalion of troops at Pengerang was the last British or Allied unit still active in the Malay Peninsula. When, on 31 January, the Johore causeway was cut, leaving only Pengerang, Tekong Island (in the Johore estuary) and Singapore still held by British Forces, the remaining planters were ordered to leave the mainland. Using the estate launch, *Miss Papan*, they had on board a total of 21 people, including some of the Asian estate staff and their families. On arrival at Changi, Martin and Browning became attached to the 2nd Malayan Infantry Brigade as intelligence and liaison officers and both volunteered for patrols 'up-country' and behind the Japanese positions.

During the next week or so, Martin made a number of landings at night on the Johore mainland, using a naval patrol boat for the crossing and rowing a dinghy when close in-shore or up-river. He visited the estate bungalow once and the estate workers' lines a number of times. All was well with the workers, but the bungalow had been quickly looted and emptied. Chinese woodcutters and 'kampong people' had, it seemed, come down in large numbers and estate workers had joined in 'when they saw stuff being carried away'. Although initially very angry, Martin saw that everything would have gone in any case and if those around had not taken things, others would have done so.

Soon, the Changi area was being dive-bombed and machine-gunned from the air and a newly mounted Japanese gun position on Pulau Ubin was hurling mortar-fire across the Strait. It became too risky to take launches up the Johore river and Paddy Martin became attached to the 1st Mysores at Pengerang. Together with Browning, his estate-deputy who had now teamed up with him again, he was involved in supplying isolated defenders on the island of Tekong with food and ammunition. These were desperate, last-minute excursions, in danger of shelling from both sides, Changi and Pulau Ubin. At Pengerang on 15 February, Martin heard that Singapore had surrended. Accompanying this radio message from headquarters was an instruction that arms had to be laid down and the arrival of the Japanese awaited.

At the time of this dramatic message, Browning happened to be a short distance away from the Pengerang base, engaged in the collection of rice. Martin hurriedly gathered together ten officers who were willing to take a chance on escaping and they made their way out of the base, crossing a land-mine field to avoid the sentry posts. In due course, the group located Browning and two companions, making a party of 13 in all. There was no pre-arranged plan as they headed on foot, in a north-east direction, in case they were pursued 'either by our own people or the Japanese'. Martin was well known in the area and he found a faithful Chinese who served as their guide. Using paths through jungle and rubber, pineapple and coconut areas, they covered 15 miles that night and lay up under cover next day, at the same time seeking contacts for the purchase of a boat. They were near Sungei Rengit, about ten miles east of Pengerang, and a boat was difficult to find, as so many had been destroyed to 'deny' them to the Japanese. But the local Chinese were very willing to help and one of them turned up with the officer of a sailing boat, just 30 feet long. The price asked for the boat was modest and Martin was ready to buy it if two Chinese would also come along to sail it and eventually return with it. The intention was to make for the Rhio group of islands, in the Dutch zone to the south of Singapore.

All was agreed and there followed another five-mile trail to the coast at Tanjong Ramunia. The boat was taken over at 8 p.m. and the escape party sailed with the tide three hours later. Their food supply consisted of eggs, condensed milk and salt. Everyone was very tired, Browning had a badly cut and festering foot, which had to be attended to, and then Martin lay in the bottom of the boat, feeling the pressure of the responsibility he had taken so far in leading this party out from the edge of captivity. He awoke in bilge water as the boat was leaking badly, so baling operations had to be organised. There was generally a good breeze in the right direction and next morning they passed the island of Bintan. On meeting small boats, they asked the way to Rhio and eventually arrived there, at the port of Tanjong Pinang.

The town was largely deserted. Dutch troops had left, shops were shut and looting had begun. Only the Dutch senior government official, the 'Controller', was left. He had three launches but said he needed them to take food to other islanders. He drew on a piece of paper a diagram of how to reach the Indragiri river in Sumatra, but what hope was there with this flimsy guidance and a leaky boat! Martin found that there was a government steamer at the jetty and decided he had to challenge the Controller, who, to do him justice, had suffered recently from the activities of looting troops. The steamer, according to its Japanese captain, was due to sail at 4 p.m. that day. Martin instructed his party to go on board (they still carried arms), paid off the Chinese who had brought the sailing boat from Johore, and waited. Soon, a number of dinghies, sampans and other small boats entered the harbour, carrying soldiers from Singapore. Many voices called out, asking to come on board the steamer and Martin replied that it was not his ship, but, so far as he was concerned, they could join it if they came quietly. By 7 p.m., when the ship finally prepared to leave, there were 60 troops on board and the

Dutch administrator conceded that they should sail direct to Sumatra. Next morning, they entered the Indragiri river; a day later,
they were trying-up at the riverside port of Rengat. Here the soldiers
joined the military organisation which was dealing with an escape
route across Sumatra.

It had been possible for Martin and his men to buy a little food at
Tanjong Pinang, but there were no stores there from which 60 men
might be fed, an obvious consideration for the Controller. Nor were
the leaders of the islanders, whom the Controller consulted, likely to
seek to delay the passage of displaced soldiers, whose discipline
might or might not be maintained. They were not to know, either,
how long it might be before Japanese advance units could arrive,
pushing south from Singapore. For Paddy Martin's Johore group it
was an achievement to have come safely so far. At Rengat, they
heard stories of the bombing and sinking of several late evacuee ships
from Singapore and realised that their sea route had been a lucky
one.

William Johnson was a canning officer in the Department of Agriculture in Johore. At a late stage in the Japanese advance he was called
upon to evacuate to Singapore and to ensure that the essential
canning machinery for which he was responsible was transferred to
the island at the same time. A proposal that it should all be moved to
Java, where canning could continue, was put to the Dutch authorities, but a week passed without a reply, by which time it was decided
that the scheme was no longer practicable because of shipping difficulties. Johnson was advised to report for duty with the Royal Navy
Volunteer Reserve, which he thought was 'leaving it a bit late', as the
Japanese were already on the island. However, he pursued the idea
to the point of seeing Admiral Spooner and found a role as sub-
lieutenant engineer on a naval ocean-going tug, the *St Breock*, which
left Singapore for Batavia on 11 February.

Two days out from port, the tug was spotted by Japanese planes
and bombed. A near-miss was effective enough to sink the vessel but
all on board ('about fifty souls' in Johnson's account) got ashore on
the island of Blakang Utang. Lieutenant Johnson was the only one
present who spoke Malay and, accompanied by another lieutenant
and a chief petty officer, he sought out people living on the island to
discuss the situation of the shipwrecked group. They were told of

another island 25 miles away where there was a Dutch administrator who would be in wireless communication with Batavia, so they set out in a Malay boat, of the dug-out canoe type, to try to establish this contact. The local Malays warned them that they would be seen and machine-gunned by Japanese aircraft, but they reached an intervening island safely by nightfall and were provided with boiled rice and a hut to sleep in by the island community. Only the mosquitoes were hostile.

Although they had lost the boat's rudder and were steering with an oar, they reached the island of Singkep on the next day and duly found the Dutch administrator to whom they reported the location and plight of the rest of their party, marooned on Blakang Utang. It was too late for the kind of communication they needed. The Dutchman had destroyed his transmitting set in anticipation of the early arrival of the Japanese and there was no ready way to send a message anywhere. The small boat crew decided, if possible, to try to make the crossing to Sumatra, though not in their present craft. While they were on Singkep, Japanese planes flew over and bombed the harbour and town of Dabo, causing much destruction and panic, and sinking the only ship of reasonable size.

On exploring the harbour area, Johnson and his colleague found two open river-going motorboats, which Johnson's engineering knowledge enabled them to get going. They left Singkep that night in the two boats, taking 12 Dutch volunteers with them, together with a supply of food contributed by these new companions. They had decided to make for the nearest point they could on the Sumatran coast, with the aid of a compass, which they salvaged from a crashed Hurricane plane on Singkep, and a school atlas, which one of them had picked up somewhere. It was a night crossing and not without some drama. One motorboat broke down and all on board had to transfer to the remaining one. This left them very overloaded and, as there was a big sea running, the Dutchmen, whose role had so far been only that of passengers, had to work furiously, baling out water for much of the night.

Two hours before dawn, they were off the Sumatran coast, but where? They waited anxiously off-shore until daylight when they were able to locate themselves a few miles south of the estuary of the Djambi river, which would offer access inland and thence in the general direction of central and western Sumatra. In much more favourable circumstances, they could hardly have made a more advantageous crossing. They found the river estuary and proceeded up-river to the town to Djambi. The motorboat which completed the journey had run continuously for 72 hours, although there had been a warning back at Singkep that it would not go for more than an hour without stopping. Had it stopped, Lieutenant Johnson recorded, 'it is pretty certain that we would all have been lost'. The boat was abandoned at Djambi and the party teamed up with a Dutch armed military convoy, heading inland and expecting to meet Japanese troops along the road. But their luck held and with the help of another lorry, and then a train, they reached Padang, travelling via Mariteboe and Solok.

The island of Singkep, at the southern end of the Rhio-Lingga chain of islands proved to be a very useful staging area for small craft making from Singapore to the eastern coast of Sumatra. Many survivors from bombing and shipwreck were gathered together at Senayang, at the northern end of the same island group and taken in hired Chinese junks to Singkep. They included some of the erstwhile passengers of the *Kuala* and the *Tun Kuang* (*Tien Kwang*), which had both been sunk off the small island of Pom Pong, 80 miles south of Singapore. The junks made conveniently for the northern side of Singkep and road transport was then found to take people to the main port at Dabo, from where a ferry service was organised to sail to the Sumatran coast and the Indragiri river. Among others who passed through Dabo in much the same way were survivors from *Fairmile*, *Grasshopper* and *Dragonfly*, all bombed or beached at Sempang on 14 February, about the same time as the *St Breock*.

When these stricken groups reached Singkep and Dabo, normal administration had largely broken down but the Dutch Controller of the island still seemed able to help with food, accommodation and valuable advice. For those fit enough to continue their travels, Singkep could only be somewhere in transit but, for many, it helped to break up long and dangerous passages by sea and to point a successful route to Sumatra. Some of those who arrived on Singkep were still thinking in terms of a destination in Java and received here the information that the Japanese navy was in the Bangka Strait and that Japanese troops had landed in the Palembang region of southern Sumatra. Loss of life on the sea routes south of Singapore was heavy enough in February 1942, but it would have been still heavier without the services provided on Singkep for those who landed there.

Like William Johnson, Peter Cardew was a last-minute Naval Reserve officer in Singapore. On 11 February, he was serving on the water-boats *Heather* and *Daisy*, based at Laburnam Quay and supplying water to ships engaged in the late evacuation. As the water-boats were shallow-draught vessels, they were also pressed into service to ferry civilians and service personnel to larger ships waiting in the Roads. For many, the water-boats were performing an essential task, but for Cardew and his colleagues it must have been rather depressing to see from their position 17 or 18 ships leaving Singapore on 12 and 13 February while they seemed to have little prospect of either a fighting role or a chance to escape from the beleagured island. A long time later they were to learn that most of the ships they had serviced and watched were bombed and sunk on the way to Java.

Late at night on 13 February, *Heather* took 50 RAF men out to one of two ships lying waiting at Singapore and returned to the quay for further instructions. They were told to expect another RAF party, 50 strong, take them aboard and then sail direct to Batavia. A Naval Commander, St Aubin, came on board to lead this adventure. *Heather* displaced about 200 tons and most of her space consisted of an enormous water-tank. Cardew wondered how 50 passengers were to be accommodated and fed on a voyage to Java. There was also a question of speed; *Heather* could manage about six knots at full speed. The voyage would be painfully slow and they could be extremely vulnerable to air attack.

As it happened, the heavy shellfire on the quay created a large bonfire area and *Heather* was given new instructions to proceed without waiting for the second RAF contingent. At 5 a.m. next morning, they joined the sister ship, *Daisy*, outside the harbour and the two boats set off together for Batavia. They had orders to hide during daylight and travel by night only, if possible, so, after three hours, *Heather* anchored into a small island just 15 miles south-west of Singapore. *Daisy* anchored two miles away, near another island, and it was agreed that they would sail separately from then onwards. Vegetation was brought from the island to camouflage *Heather*, the islanders themselves helping with the work. Japanese planes were overhead throughout the daylight hours, but *Heather* was not attacked; *Daisy* was bombed twice, but not hit.

Heather sailed again at about 5 p.m. and reached the island of Singkep at noon next day (15 February). By this time, it had emerged that a large bomb splinter was lodged in the compass, this probably occurred when they were still in Singapore, and it was a relief to be given some navigational charts by Dutch officers on Singkep. Trying to keep to a routine, they left the island at about 5 p.m. for another night's sailing, this time in the direction of Bangka Strait and Batavia.

When they had gone a short distance, *Heather's* crew saw a light flashing from the shore. The Dutch were signalling that they should heave-to and send a man ashore, which they did. The message was that news had just come over the wireless that Japanese troops had landed at Palembang and that Bangka Strait was full of the Japanese navy. The Commander accepted Dutch advice, which was to abandon any ideas of reaching Java and turn instead towards the Sumatran coast; the Djambi river estuary was the new objective. It was too late to reach there by early next morning, so another group of islands was chosen to provide the daytime hideout. Unfortunately, time was lost at the end of the next day, when *Heather* was stuck fast on the mud and could not be moved until 2 a.m. the following morning at high tide. This meant another day of hiding, one on which a Japanese cruiser passed within a mile of the boat and its hiding place, without spotting it under the camouflage.

At last, on 18 February, they reached the estuary of the Djambi river and steamed up river to find *Daisy* on the river, but abandoned, with her sea cocks open. Catching up later with *Daisy's* crew, they learned that their sister ship had arrived at Singkep shortly after them and had also made for the Djambi river, going ahead, no doubt, while the others were stuck on the mudbank. *Daisy's* crew had accepted an opportunity to transfer to a British naval launch to speed their way up-river and hence the abandoned boat. When they reached the town of Djambi, about 150 miles up-river, the *Heather* party was called upon by Dutch officials to give up their boat in exchange for a launch which was just big enough to take the 13 men, provided they were restricted to one piece of luggage each, which meant dumping some of their possessions carried so far. Although they accepted the situation, Peter Cardew's view was that *Heather*, which had a draught of only about five feet, could still have contined up-river without problems. As it was, the launch itself broke down next day, with a broken water-pump, and the *Heather* men found themselves bargaining with a Chinese bus-owner to give him two rifles and some ammunition in exchange for the loan of his bus! This also turned out to be not the best of deals, for the bus broke down 20 miles further on.

In what must have seemed an anti-climax situation, but, as will appear, not untypical of what could sometimes happen on the way to Padang, the *Heather* crew lost their independence when picked up by a Dutch military convoy, which took them to the small town of Mariteboe, another 150 miles inland. It was 20 February, and about a week since they had left Singapore. In Mariteboe, there were nearly 200 other refugees, mostly army personnel whose ships, in some cases, had been sunk. Cardew and his companions were ready for at least a short rest, with the Dutch here largely providing food and making the transport arrangements. By noon next day, four buses and two lorries had arrived to take all the refugees by road in the direction of Padang

At this stage, and for a short period, the experiences of William Johnson and Peter Cardew seem to have overlapped. Both reached Djambi, where Johnson's party abandoned their motorboat ad proceeded by road with a Dutch military convoy and Cardew's party, perhaps reluctantly, gave up their water boat. Both reached Mariteboe, possibly with the same army convoy, though Cardew's group, meanwhile, had short experiences with a Dutch launch and a Chinese-owned bus. Neither group was kept waiting long in Mariteboe.

Among those who passed through the island of Singkep in escaping form Singapore were some of the members of the staff of the Federated Malay States Railways. On Friday 13 February, a party of named members of railway staff, with permission to leave Singapore, passed through the gates of the Teluk Ayer basin and was taken by launch to board HMS *Grasshopper*. They joined a number of other civilians on board, together with some naval and military personnel and nine Japanese prisoners; estimates of the total number of passengers have varied widely and there is some evidence to suggest that the ship's captain had no clear instructions concerning the evacuees. *Grasshopper* left at about 7 p.m. but, after steaming for two hours, had orders to return to embark more people. Regular shelling of the docks delayed further sailing until 12.30 a.m. on the 14th.

At daylight, *Grasshopper* was sailing in company with two other vessels on rescue and evacuation missions, *Dragonfly* and *Fairmile*. At 8.30 a.m., a single Japanese plane bombed the ships unsuccessfully, but, two hours later, a large number of bombers appeared and made persistent attacks on the three ships. *Dragonfly* was sunk, *Fairmile* escaped, but only to run ashore and beach on a nearby island, Pulau Sempang. *Grasshopper* was hit by a bomb which passed through the petty officer's mess and exploded below, killing a number of servicemen and wounding others; the ship then caught fire. Manoeuvring all the time, the ship's captain managed to avoid any further direct hits, but near-misses also caused damage and, eventually, he ran close to Sempang and ordered 'abandon ship'. They were about 200 yards from the shore and the women and wounded were taken off in floats in one of the ship's boats. The wounded included 13 stretcher cases, two of whom, both servicemen, died during the night. Japanese bombers followed up their attack by machine-gunning the stranded ship and the beach to which the passengers struggled. *Grasshopper* blew up that night and became, in the words of W. F. Wegener, a senior railway engineer, 'a blackened and twisted hulk'.

The survivors from this episode found themselves on an island 130 miles from Singapore and without food and water. A move was made to neighbouring island, Sungei Buoya, though it took 24 hours for some of the wounded to reach there. The next initiative was to ferry people, starting with the wounded, to the island of Singkep, where they were taken by buses and lorries to the capital, Dabo. Here, the wounded were sent to hospital, women were accommodated in the houses of Dutch officials, probably recently vacated, and hostel accommodation was found for the men. Large numbers of troops continued to arrive on the island in the next few days; some were housed in the Dabo Club and others in Malay-type houses. On 20 February, separate organisation was arranged for civilian, and Services survivors, none of whom knew how long they would be on the island, and all of whom had to be fed. Rice, dried fish and vegetables provided the staple diet, and not very much of it, with an occasional piece of bread. Gradually, however, the numbers were reduced by the ferrying of groups to the Sumatran coast and access to the Indragiri River. As so often, night sailings were made to avoid the attention of Japanese aircraft. Mr Wegener, of the railways' staff, made the crossing on a tank landing barge in the company of naval and air force personnel, Japanese prisoners with their guards and interpreters, and some Indian, Malay and Chinese survivors of ships which had been sunk.

There were others who had cause to remember Singkep with gratitude. Flying Officer R. Dennis Dodds left Singapore on 13 February, on board HMS *Trang*. With the ship's company they were carrying perhaps 80 people in all, mostly military. After about two hours, the vessel developed boiler trouble and was grounded at St John's Island. Dodds found a damaged RAF launch in the vicinity and worked until it seemed possible to use it. On Sunday 15 February, the launch set out, towing the two lifeboats from *Trang*. It was another slow, island-stopping exercise, the party hiding and sleeping as circumstances allowed. Threading through the archipelago, they reached the island of Lingga on the 19th and, two days later, set out for Singkep, reduced to rowing as they reached Dabo on the 22nd. There were still many refugees on Singkep and Flying Officer Dodd's party no doubt needed a short rest; some would have been in need of hospital treatment. But these were anxious days, as time was running out for any regular ferrying between Singkep and Sumatra. On 26 February, Dodds negotiated with the local owner of a launch to take a party across to Sumatra; that night, they made the crossing, arriving on the Sumatran coast at about 4 a.m., and at Perigi Raja, on the Indragiri River, three hours later. The launch towed a large river-barge and Dodds recalled later meeting 'a tall Australian captain, known as the Pirate', who seemed to be in charge of the river operation. This man can hardly have been anyone other than William Reynolds, who became almost a legendary figure in the rescue operations among the islands.

William Reynolds had been a shipmaster who, in his own words, 'after years of wandering had gravitated to Hong Kong'. From there, he captained ships taking part in the annual Muslim pilgrimage to Jiddah, and thence to Mecca, on vessels carrying on through to Genoa and Barcelona. On the return voyage, his ship would pick up the pilgrims and return them to Singapore, Java and other places. With this experience, he came to know the 'Dutch Archipelago' very well, but in 1925, he gave up the sea, settled in Perak, Malaya, and worked in tin mining.

During the short, dramatic period of the Japanese advance in Malaya, he joined up with the Royal Engineers in Northern Command and was allocated to the 3rd Field Company, Bombay Sappers and Miners, as an expert in demolition. He came south with the Company, blowing up tin-dredges, mining machinery and bridges and generally assisting the 'scorched earth' policy in the path of the invader. Finally, he arrived in Singapore on 19 January, and went

round looking for jobs, but nobody seemed to want him, 'least of all
the navy'. He found in the harbour about 30 Japanese fishing boats,
all equipped with diesel engines, and offered to try to put them in
order, but was again rebuffed. By 10 February, Reynolds realised
that Singapore was likely to fall and he took matters into his own
hands. He chose eight Chinese from a local boarding house, took
them down to the harbour at Teluk Ayer and, selecting the best of
the fishing boats, set his party to work reconditioning her. Working
through the day and night and finding fuel oil and other necessary
stores and foodstuffs, they had the little 70-foot-long boat ready for
the sea on the evening of 11 February. Next morning, they sailed for
the island of Blakang Mati with the intention of taking off as many as
possible of the Volunteers billeted at the Straits Trading Company's
works. Before they could reach the island, 27 Japanese bombers
came over and dropped high explosives, so Reynolds changed direction and made for St John's Island. Whilst there for a few hours, he
gave directions to passing motorboats and other small craft on their
way out from Singapore, but, by 1 p.m., following further bombing in
the area, he decided to make eastwards to Rhio and avoid what
seemed to be a dangerous exodus through the Durian Strait. He
arrived at Rhio on the evening of the 12th and was ordered by the
Dutch authorities to anchor. Next morning, Rhio was bombed by two
Japanese planes. There were said to be no casualties but, in the
knowledge that there were a lot of wives and children of the Dutch-
Indonesian garrison soldiers on the island, Reynolds offered to help
with their evacuation. What he described as 'an old broken down
island vessel' lay beside the wharf, bearing the name *Silver Gull*.
Taking 216 women and children on this vessel, and crowding another
50 on his own deck, he set off, taking the *Silver Gull* in tow and
making for the Indragiri river in central Sumatra. They sailed
through the night and put in to a small island at dawn for fear of air
attack. The passengers disembarked and rested through the day
under trees and foliage, while Reynolds and his crew took on a very
necessary supply of fresh water. Another night's sailing brought them
to the mouth of the Indragiri river in Amphitrite Bay and the tow
continued to hold up-river to a tiny wharf some 30 miles from
Rengat. Here the passengers disembarked, to be taken by lorry to
Rengat, and *Silver Gull* was left berthed. After a short break,
Reynolds and his crew took their boat up-river also to Rengat.

In conversation with the Dutch Resident and officials at Rengat,
Reynolds learned that a number of wounded were on the island of

Pom Pong, about 160 miles away. As quickly as possible, he commandeered mattresses, blankets and foodstuffs, and, at 2 a.m. next morning (it was now 16 February), the former Japanese fishing boat (wearing Chinese colours) was on its way down to the sea and bound for Pom Pong. Most of the sea voyage took place at night, with arrival in the Pom Pong area in the early hours of 17 February. A total of 76 people was embarked here from the survivors of three wrecked ships, nine were badly wounded and suffering greatly; a nursing sister accompanied them back to Sumatra. Leaving these refugees at Tembilahan on the Indragiri river, where there was a Malay hospital, Reynolds set out again to pick up more of the Pom Pong victims. Meanwhile, an Australian army surgeon performed seven major operations that night in Tembilahan.

On the second rescue mission to the Pom Pong area, Reynolds took off 96 people, many of them formerly on the staff of the Public Works Department in Malaya. This group was also taken back to Tembilahan in the fishing smack which now proceeded further to Rengat. In a long letter written in Australia in May 1943, William Reynolds described all these movements but it is difficult to follow him in detail after the Pom Pong period. He was continuously on the move for many days and claimed altogether to have visited the islands of Moro, Benko, Singkep and Lingga, as well as Pom Pong, 'Malay fishermen, by arrangement, bringing stragglers to these rendezvous, where we picked them up'. On 6 March, at the request of a Dutch Resident, he undertook an espionage trip, visiting Tanjong Pinang (Rhio), Tanjong Bali (Karimoen) and Tanjong Batu (Koendoer). Near Tanjong Pinang, they engaged a Japanese patrol vessel which, allegedly, withdrew. At Tanjong Batu, the Chinese crew deserted to join a large Chinese community there, leaving only Reynolds and two other men to handle the ship. Returning via the north of Singkep to Sumatra, Reynolds and his colleagues learned that Japanese troops were approaching from the south of the island and were reported to be only ten miles away, coming from Djambi. They were given instructions to proceed to sea, in case they were captured. Even on the last return trip to the Indragiri, they picked up a number of men on small craft *en route*. In so doing, they may well have saved further lives, but for any people left in Sumatra it was too late to escape capture by the Japanese. Altogether, Reynolds claimed to have transported more than 1500 people from the smaller islands to Sumatra, where many would have the chance to cross to the west coast and the hope of a ship to freedom. The numbers seem impossi-

ble to check, but there is no doubt about the range of his rescue
work.

Alex Niven, an engineer of the Public Works Department in Malaya
was among those bombed on the *Kuala* and marooned on the island
of Pom Pong. Together with most of his colleagues who shared this
experience he was eventually picked up by William Reynolds in the
powered fishing boat and taken across to Sumatra. In a letter to his
wife, Eileen, written in June 1942 (when she was in Australia and he
was in India), he described his feelings at leaving Pom Pong. 'We
were supremely thankful,' he wrote, 'to be heading for Sumatra,
some forty odd miles away, even though we knew by now that the
Japanese were there and were patrolling the Straits which we had to
cross.' He commented that there had been no lifeboats or lifesavers
of any kind on the fishing vessel, but the refugees on board were not
feeling too depressed. Some, including himself, had spent a week on
Pom Pong, during which time Singapore had fallen and Japanese
attacks had been made on Java and southern Sumatra. They realised
that any chance now of getting to Batavia was 'definitely hopeless';
they were happy to settle for the possibility of eventually reaching the
west coast of Sumatra.

As they were still in open waters next morning when they had
expected to be on the Indragiri river, a hasty camouflage arrangement was necessary. Over the ropes, which ran horizontally from the
roof of the wheelhouse to the mast, they draped blankets and bed
sheets. When planes were heard, or the 'spotter' yelled 'aircraft' they
pulled the blankets and sheets out to form inverted 'V' shape, took
cover underneath and left the Chinese helmsman sitting cross-legged
on top of the wheelhouse. To any inquisitive aircraft they aimed to
give the appearance of a Chinese fishing smack with a sunshade up
and some washing on the line. It was by no means the only situation
at sea in which this tactic, with a little variety of detail, was employed
for exactly the same reason.

Niven estimated that the estuary of the Indragiri was at least two
miles wide, the river with its brown, muddy waters, being tidal for a
considerable distance inland. He thought they would never see the
rooves of the first village along the river, Perigi Raja, which was their
first objective, but, eventually, they did glimpse the typical

'kampong'-type dwellings. They were dismayed subsequently to find the village lifeless and deserted, but there was nothing to be gained by stopping. They carried on 45 miles inland to the small township of Tembilahan, which they reached in the late afternoon. Here, two disused godowns by the riverside were designated by the Dutch authorities as temporary accommodation for those passing through.

Among the many who passed this way was Engineers' Captain C. O. Jennings. He left Singapore in a party of 25 men who commandeered a Chinese junk, the *Hiap Hin*, and sailed at 4 a.m. on 16 February, the day after the surrender. It was a late and bold bid to escape and, inevitably, it rested on support from islands in the archipelago. Provisions were obtained from a small island at an early stage, then the junk sailed on to the island of Moro, picking up four soldiers from a dinghy *en route*. Moro island served as a base for the official organisation which had been set up to help escapers. Tin boxes held there contained provisions for 20 men for four days, consisting of food and other necessities. A small guiding group was expected to be found there, helping with directions to the Indragiri river.

At Moro, Captain Jennings found 130 men from Singapore, most of whom had rowed small boats; their hands were sore and several of them were wounded. All but three men, who stayed behind on Moro, were taken aboard the junk, which made the passage safely to Sumatra, and then inland to Tembilahan, where hospital cases were left. A change of river transport was needed here and an invasion barge, the *Plover*, and a river launch each towed a string of two boats. As another 130 men embarked at Tembilahan, the total number engaged in this exercise was approaching 300. As movement from Singapore came to focus on Sumatra, large numbers of people needed food and rest along the way and many needed medical treatment. What had typically started out as a series of separate enterprises, many of a very individual kind, came to be shaped by a blend of military and civil administration. British army officers generally provided the military contribution and Dutch administrators the civil element, though Dutch military transport also became involved. It was a complex and difficult task for those assisting with the organisation and was by no means always welcomed or appreciated by those who were being organised. Delays along the route inevitably increased tension and produced complaints. The goal for those on the Sumatra escape route was Padang on the west coast and its associated port, known as Emmahaven. Those who made for Padang were inclined, at times, to chafe at delay, though none in fact knew what to expect at their journey's end; the end, really, of another stage of their journey. There were inevitable delays and frustrations and, finally, inevitable disappointments. Yet, in retrospect, it is perhaps remarkable that so many people, military and civilian, successfully crossed the difficult terrain of central Sumatra from east coast to west coast. Certainly, it was no tourist trip.

Sergeant-Major E. C. Hosking of the Royal Army Ordnance Corps was stationed in Kuala Lumpur when the Japanese invaded Malaya and he was quickly moving north to organise the withdrawal of some ammunition trucks from Taiping to south of Ipoh. He was caught in the railway goodsyard at Ipoh when it was bombed, with great explosions, but soon back in further transport work, moving stores from Kuala Lumpur. Subsequently, he was withdrawn to Singapore, where he arrived on 28 December 1941. Here, he was occupied clearing the docks of vehicles, issuing components to repair damaged ones and performing general workshop duties. 'It was not,' as he recalled, 'a first-class job, but better than being idle at corps HQ.'

The bombing of the docks area increased through January and, on the 16th, he saw his wife and children leave for Australia on SS *Narkunda*. The Ordnance workshop operated under increasingly difficult and dangerous conditions and the local fitters simply stayed away. Hosking must have been wondering what was in store for him at the end when, on 12 February, he was ordered to join a small first party which would set up a base workshop in Java. There were 27 of them in all, including two officers and 18 warrant officers and NCOs; they were taken in a small launch to SS *Jarak*, normally a Straits Steamship Company coaster of about 300 tons but now being used as a minesweeper; some of the naval crew were survivors from *Repulse* and *Prince of Wales*.

They anchored overnight and moved out at dawn on 13 February. A smoke haze hid the dwindling view of Singapore. By 9 a.m., they were at anchor again, this time taking shelter in a creek between two islands as waves of Japanese bombers flew overhead; one gave them a burst of machine-gun fire. In the evening, they were moving again, the captain's intention was to make for Palembang for stores and water. They were off the Sumatran coast at daybreak on 14 February, but facing white beaches and mangrove swamps, with no shelter visible. Within a few hours, they were spotted by a Japanese reconnaissance plane and, shortly after, the masts of naval ships were seen, three Japanese cruisers and one destroyer. In a tense and hectic spell *Jarak* avoided 20 or 30 salvoes from 6-inch guns and then a large sea-plane bomber dropped first one bomb and then another on them, both near-misses. *Jarak*'s gun, a Lewis-gun, and rifles blazed defiance.

The minesweeper now made for a small group of islands, about eight miles ahead, with the Japanese destroyer following at full speed and firing a 4-inch salvo from a distance of about 2000 yards. One shell hit the bridge and port side of *Jarak*, while others struck the forward hold (the magazine) and the starboard side plating. Sergeant-Major Hosking was badly wounded as a large splinter entered his thigh, and there were other casualties as the captain ordered 'abandon ship'. Despite further shelling, two boats were lowered successfully and as they were rowed away in a very rough sea the destroyer and the seaplane left the scene. It was very cold, the sea was constantly coming into the boats and Hosking was suffering badly from his wound and had to be kept warm. He still helped those in his own boat by giving advice on the rigging-up of a sail, using an oar as mast.

Eventually, they reached the group of islands they had seen and went ashore on the rocks of the main one at midnight. There were coconuts here and, next day, spring water was found. To their surprise, the shipwrecked men could still see the *Jarak* afloat in the distance and one of the naval officers took out a small party to try to retrieve the ship, or at least some of the stores. They pumped out the engine-room and, using all the wood they could find, got up steam and brought the ship round to the island that evening. It was a very successful operation, but they had lost one of their two lifeboats in carrying it out; all now seemed to depend on the *Jarak*. The bombers and the seaplane were back again next morning (16 February), the plane machine-gunning the ship and the jungle area behind the beach. As the men had dispersed round the island there were no casualties and Hosking, unable to move on his own, felt safe under the cover of a rock where he had been placed.

That evening, a party of stokers rowed the remaining boat out to where the ship lay and worked to get steam up again while a quarter-master sergeant of the RAOC, who accompanied them, managed to repair the ship's wireless. This party returned to shore with the news that Singapore had fallen and the Japanese were occupying Palembang. It was now decided that they should try to reach the estuary of the Indragiri river in Sumatra and steam up-river as far as Rengat. Like other rescue vessels in the area, *Jarak* was driven hard to achieve a successful night crossing, but the pressure was now too much for the engines, the bearings ran out and, in the early hours of the morning (17 February), the ship ran aground on the island of Singkep. Later that day, the ship's stores were carried to the beach and *Jarak* was taken out and scuttled. As members of the shipwrecked party must soon have realised, they might have fared much worse than land on Singkep. They were able to contact Malay seamen whose sailing boats took them round the coast to Dabo, the only town of any size on the island and a gathering-place for hundreds of others, escapees and evacuees from Malaya and Singapore, mostly survivors from bombing and shipwreck.

Sergeant-Major Hosking's leg wound had become very dirty and foul and he feared his only chance of living might be to have it sawn off. But, at Dabo, Captain Kirkwood, an Indian army medical officer, looked after him, removed the shell splinter from his leg and syringed the hole. In many other cases, the doctor was busy with amputations of gangrenous limbs. The nurses in the Dabo hospital were themselves victims of bombing at sea, yet were working devotedly for the care of others. A former water-boat from the Singapore front, *Heather*, rigged up as a hospital launch, took about 80 patients, including Hosking, to Sumatra, where they were housed in a Dutch hospital at Djambi, and 'very kindly treated'. On 27 February, the day after their arrival, the more lightly wounded patients left in buses for Padang, but the stretcher cases, including Hosking, were to be retained for a few days before following them. Time was running out. Japanese troops were approaching from further south and, on 1 March, a late attempt vas made to get the rest of the sick and wounded evacuees away by bus. They were, in the event unable to make the crossing of a river where the ferry had been destroyed by Dutch troops to delay the Japanese advance. So, it was back to Djambi, where the Japanese arrived on 3 March.

Fortunately, Sergeant-Major Hosking's wound healed. The war now entered another long phase for him as a prisoner-of-war in Palembang, then, briefly, back to Singapore and finally to camps in

Taiwan, following long, miserable voyages, spent mostly in the holds of ships.

———————

Squadron Leader T. C. Carter, Senior RAF Radio Officer, Singapore was in charge of the last party of RAF men to leave the island. They and others in their unit had been working with what was known, and not known to many, as RDF, or Range and Direction Finding Equipment; it was soon to be known as 'radar' and with the RAF its prime function was aircraft detection. Since the equipment and its use on the British side was still very secret, terminology was deliberately used to confuse. Thus, radar stations were known for a time as AMES (Air Ministry Experimental Stations) with a number attached, and a Radio Branch in the RAF, as distinct from a Signals Branch, specifically had the responsibility for RDF (radar) stations and their equipment and personnel. At the time of the Japanese invasion of Malaya, some 550 RAF officers and men of the Radio Branch were stationed in Malaya and Singapore. What Squadron Leader Carter was to describe as 'the jewel in the radar crown' was No. 243 AMES, a Transportable Unit (TRU) originally based at Mersing on the east coast of Johore, about 70 miles north of Singapore. His own unit, the Radio Installation and Maintenance Unit (RIMU) was on Singapore island and had the responsibility of providing technical support for the radar stations and also administering them.

As the Japanese army advanced into Johore, radar stations were withdrawn to Singapore and their equipment was overhauled at RIMU; later, the same procedure followed in the more limited environment of the island itself. Some stations and their crews were sent to Java along with about half of RIMU and also the staff of the Filter Room, another Singapore installation. As Senior Radio Officer on the island, T. C. Carter stayed there with what was left, which included the rump of the Radio Installation and Maintenance Unit and a very mobile 243 AMES which became based first near Tengah, then east of the city and Kallang aerodrome (the Japanese having by this time overrun Tengah) and finally at a location west of Fort Canning and the Cathay Building. The equipment now needed significant repairs and the re-erection of the masts, work estimated to take 48 hours. It was too late, for the island was on the verge of surrender.

It was in these circumstances that Squadron Leader Carter organised a demolition party to destroy, thoroughly, all remaining RAF radar equipment on Singapore island, including the much travelled 243 AMES. Demolition had to be thorough to prevent anything of a secret nature falling into Japanese hands and sledge hammers were used, followed by petrol. It was equally important that RAF personnel who had been working in the Radio Branch should be accorded special protection and assistance to leave Singapore. As T. C. Carter recorded, all radio personnel were acutely aware of the extreme importance of preserving the secrecy of the RDF and of the ruthlessness of the Japanese military police. He obtained the necessary permission to get all remaining RAF Radio men away in boats, including those who had formed the demolition party. All were taken out to little ships, the last man being the Squadron Leader himself, who in the pattern of time and movement was separated from his men and boarded the *Shu Kwang*, a Shanghai steamship of 788 tons, in the ownership of the Asiatic Petroleum Company, but now on war service under naval orders. This ship left Singapore at dawn on 14 February.

It was a desperately dangerous time to be sailing and many ships had been sunk by bombers on the previous day. In the early afternoon of 14 February, the *Shu Kwang*, unarmed and slow in the open sea, was attacked twice by Japanese bombers. In a vivid description T. C. Carter recalled that the first attack was made by twin-engined aircraft flying straight and level in formation; bombs damaged the ship below the water-line. The second attack, more terrifying, was by dive-bombers. According to naval sources, 11 of the 273 passengers were killed and 40 wounded, many seriously. They were left afloat, but slowly sinking. Those who, like the RAF Radio Unit men, had faced death many times recently on the Malayan mainland and in Singapore and were then taken off in small ships like the *Shu Kwang*, must have felt, as did Squadron Leader Carter, that they had reached their lowest point when those planes attacked the crowded ships, treating them 'like practice targets'.

Shu Kwang remained afloat, but was sinking 'slowly when the aircraft disappeared and, astonishingly, other small vessels came to the rescue. First the two ships' boats which were still serviceable were used, then the *Tanjong Pinang* and *Tenggaroh* (the Sultan of Kedah's yacht) took off survivors, together with *Pengail* (in the naval account), which took wounded and three Malay ratings. In the words of T. C. Carter, 'it seemed like a miracle'.

On the *Tanjong Pinang*, the Squadron Leader met up again with some of the Radio Unit men. Their ship had actually sailed before his, but stuck on a sandback outside Singapore harbour. For those on board the *Shu Kwang* this was a great stroke of luck as the *Pinang* played a major part in their rescue; in fact, Squadron Leader Carter considered that only the *Tenggaroh* and the *Tanjong Pinang* actually came alongside the stricken ship. What followed can be briefly told. *Shu Kwang* was abandoned (sunk by gunfire from *Tanjong Pinang* according to the naval record), but its passengers reached Sumatra. T. C. Carter conducted his own group across the island to reach Padang; RAF survivors from each of a number of other small ships, joined him, to make a total of 28 survivors. They were at Padang at the right time. British navy destroyers and cruisers called by chance, looking for fuel, and they carried away many refugees from Singapore. The RAF party mostly reached Colombo on a naval cruiser and three other RAF men arrived there from Sumatra on a Dutch freighter. T. C. Carter calculated that, out of some 40 officers and 500 men who had manned the RDF in the Far East, only two officers and 29 airmen reached Ceylon.

Mr. M. C. Hay was officiating as Chief Inspector of Mines in the Federated Malay States at the outbreak of the Japanese war and was also in training with a light artillery unit in the FMS Volunteers. By mid-December 1941, he was on active service with field guns. Like much of the rest of the defending forces in Malaya, he was often on the move. Starting from Perak, the Light Battery in which he served was stationed at Kuala Selangor in early January 1942, then, some two weeks later, at Pontian Kechil in south-west Johore. Hearing that the Japanese had taken Batu Pahat, the gunners expected enemy attacks down the coast road, but none came. Instead, the Battery moved to a new position on the beach, dug the guns in and sandbagged them, only to receive orders to move the same night. On 27 and 28 January they were retreating to Johore Bahru, and then across the causeway to Singapore.

The Light Battery took up a number of positions on Singapore island as part now of 88th Field Regiment. At one stage they were directing fire on points east of Johore Bahru and later they put down a barrage on the Thompson village area to harass the invaders. By 12

February, they had taken up their final gun position by Monk's Hill School, just north of Government House. On the morning of 15 February, they were themselves subjected to a heavy bombardment and the upper storey of the adjacent school building was largely wrecked. In the afternoon they received an order to put the guns out of action and destroy instruments and documents; a surrender was imminent. As the Battery did not have space to blow up its guns, the gunners damaged the breach blocks, at the same time smashing instruments, dial sights and ranger tables, and destroying maps and documents. A final order came to the effect that they should stay in position until the Japanese arrived.

This was the point at which Lance-Bombardier (as he was) Hay together with a Sergeant Ross and Gunners Wilkes, Harvey and H. R. Ross began their attempt to escape. They made for the road behind the school, then on to Orchard Road, where they saw lorries and cars full of troops racing down the road and others making their way on foot. It was after 5 p.m. but they noticed the flag still flying on Fort Canning and, for a short time, joined another artillery unit. But the situation was obviously hopeless and, with three more soldiers added to their number, the little party walked to Clifford Pier. There were many other soldiers wandering around, but the members of this small groups stayed together, hoping this would give them a better chance of escaping.

Entering the New Reclamation area, they made their way along the sea-wall to a landing stage where they hoped they might find a sampan. When they found one, they also found some senior military officers in attendance, namely, the Australian Major-General Gordon-Bennett, his Staff Major, Clark Moses, and his ADC, Captain Walker. A Chinese man had guided the officers to this point but was unwilling to go any further. In Mr. Hay's account, the General had in mind the idea of crossing to Johore, then finding a way to Malacca in the hope that a large enough vessel might be found there in which to cross to Sumatra. In the event, all agreed to look for a sailing vessel in Singapore harbour and attempt a crossing to Sumatra directly from there. In the urgent search for a suitable boat, there were differences to be resolved about speedy departure, on the General's side, and on ensuring the whole party with Mr Hay stayed together. Eventually, they made their way by small boat to three junks lying at anchor and boarded one of them; already there were some British army officers and other ranks on board. The Chinese captain and his crew were not very anxious to sail, at least not until the next morning, but a combined tactic of removing the captain's smoking materials until after they had sailed, and a payment to him of 100 dollars by Gordon-Bennet changed the situation and they left at 12·30 a.m. on 16 February, making towards Pulau Samboe. Within two or three hours, they were lying off this island and negotiations were in hand for an agreement to sail the junk to Sumatra. At Pulau Bulang, the captain went ashore to pick up a supply of opium for the journey and located a Chinese pilot for the main crossing, a man who offered to provide this service for 20 dollars and accepted a down-payment of half the sum.

Two soldiers, one Australian and the other British, came aboard from a sampan, each with his own story to tell. The Briton, an AA gunner, had been cut off when the Japanese captured Pasir Panjang, west of the city area of Singapore, and had subsequently escaped in a fishing boat; the Australian had managed to make his way from the island of Blakang Mati, via Pulau Samboe, and had swum part of the way. These new arrivals brought the total number in the party of escapers to 21, only half of whom had brought food or water. The pilot threaded his way among the islands but it became noticeable that his direction was mainly east-north-east, whereas the main bearing should have been south-west. Hay and others who knew something about sailing saw several tempting channels to the south-west and asked the pilot why he didn't follow them, a question which was met with excuses until they decided to put him downstairs and take over the navigation themselves.

It was slow going, as they were only making five knots and they called at an island for fruit and water. They were also constantly aware of the possible danger from Japanese aircraft, so they left only one or two men on the deck, wearing Chinese hats, in the daytime; the rest all hid below. On 18 February, they were off the Sumatran coast, south of Kampar and, on the next day, Gordon-Bennett and his staff transferred to a motor-launch manned by Australians and went their own way. The General was soon to escape by air from Sumatra. The junk reached the estuary of the Indragiri at about daybreak on 20 February and, following advice from a Dutch naval patrol, proceeded up-river to Tembilahan. It was now five days since they had left Singapore. The junk's skipper was paid another 50 dollars, money which had been left for the purpose by Gordon-Bennett, and money was raised to pay a few dollars each for the crew. Apart from the strange aberrations of the pilot hired *en route*, the Chinese junk and its crew had served the escapers very well, even to the point of sharing their scanty stores of rice and coffee.

From Tembilahan onwards, M. C. Hay and those with him were in
the hands of British officers and Dutch officials organising transport
and transit camps across Sumatra to the west coast. They reached
Padang on 27 February and, two days later, were taken on board
HMS *Tenedos*, a British destroyer, and transferred to HMS *Danae*, a
British cruiser, which reached Colombo on 5 March. From the
Sumatran coast and onwards up-river, they had enjoyed the welcome
help of a Malay pilot, and by this time they had seen several junks
and launches, 'full of escaped personnel'.

As late as 16 February 1942, H. C. Vanburen of the Federated
Malay States Volunteer Forces left the island of Blakang Mati in a
local boat with a small military group of ten men. Half of them were
Volunteers and the rest regular soldiers, based on the island. Aware
of the dangers from mines and spotter aircraft, they planned initially
to make for a neighbouring island and covered their skins with black
jettisoned oil hoping to give the appearance of local fishermen. At
their first island call, they were fortunate enough to be able to
purchase a sail and, encouraged by the faster movement which they
could now achieve, they continued their voyage on the same day. All
was well until the wind suddenly dropped and it was back to the oars
again, and a struggle to make a further island by nightfall. Two of the
men in the party had decided to stay behind on the first island, so
they were down to eight.

A striking feature of this small-boat adventure, and of several
others like it; was the generosity and all-round assistance which the
escapers received from island fisherfolk; both Malays and Chinese.
On the second island, Vanburen and his party were joined at a
cooked evening meal by a few fishermen who gave guidance about
times and tides and the direction they should make for. They left next
day with full water bottles and a healthy supply of coconuts. Yet
there was nothing easy about this voyage. Calm conditions prevailed
and for the next two or three days there was much hard rowing to be
done by an inexperienced crew.

Another small, and apparently deserted, island provided an overnight base, and the following day's exploration revealed a small
diesel-engined craft beached in shallow water in a sheltered bay.
With all hands helping, it was not too difficult to float this vessel and
fuel was found in the tank. The challenge was to start the engine; this
Mr Vanburen achieved, to everyone's surprise and joy. How to
secure enough fuel and cross the Durian Strait to Sumatra was the

next problem. At anchor, a mile out at sea, lay a burnt-out coastal steamer and it was decided that a few of the party would make a trial run to this wreck, in search of fuel. They reached the ship and tied up alongside in the shadowed area, to lessen the chances of being spotted from the air. They were in luck as they found several drums of diesel oil and, for a bonus, three bottles of Bols gin. But, on board there was a tragic and distressing scene. It was a ship which had caught fire after being bombed, and Bob Vanburen recalled that the stench from burnt bodies was so overpowering that the boarding party could not stay long.

Meanwhile, one of the men left on the island had located an islander family on the opposite side from where the escapers had landed and he now chose to stay with them. As he was the party's principal Malay speaker, this was disconcerting, but it had to be recognised that every stage with small boats on the open seas brought a fresh challenge, face-to-face with unknown hazards of time, distance, weather and enemy action. It was no rowing boat which the escapers were now handling, so when the engine stopped, after about two hours, they faced the prospect of floating in the open sea, and in full daylight. Using a dim oil-lamp and such tool-kit as had been found on the vessel, Vanburen worked desperately to re-start the engine. After what he called 'a couple of hours of trial and error system', he 'struck lucky and had the engine firing again'.

Heading in the direction of the Sumatran coast that morning, they made for a large complex of off-shore fishing stakes, with shelters on stilts to house a mainly fishing community. This was another very welcome stroke of good fortune as the small party was made welcome and allowed to rest here and, on payment of a small fee, provided with two guides when they left. Despite this measure of help and security, the rest of the sea-journey still seemed very long as they chugged slowly past islands and inlets. Their probable overall route lay via Batan, Bulan, Tyiombol and Durian. Eventually, they arrived in a large bay, the entrance to the River Indragiri, which was the gateway into the road system of Sumatra for so many refugees. In the early reaches of the river one further problem occurred. A piece of heavy driftwood jammed in the propellor and the propellor shaft bent slightly on the sudden stoppage of the engine. A repair, which could not be handled on board, became necessary. Fortunately, just at the right time, a local Malay appeared from the jungle and suggested that two of them carried the shaft to a village to which he would guide them. Here, ten minutes away, his friend, the local blacksmith, got his forge going, using bellows made of bamboo tubes, heated the metal and hammered it straight. The party was soon on its way again and that evening, they reached Rengat, where they became part of what some were to call 'the organisation'.

A Malay suddenly appeared from a larger boat tied up at the riverside just in front of theirs and wanted to know what they were doing with his boat! They told him that they were pleased they could now deliver it to him. The rest of this story can be briefly told. Motor-trucks took the party, and many others, to the rubber plantation transit camp at Ayer Molek, then, after a couple of days, it was a further full day's road journey to Padang, where they arrived just at the right time to be picked up by the navy, in H. C. Vanburen's case, HMAS *Hobart*. At Colombo, he succeeded in joining a troopship taking Australians to the defence of their homeland. Only two months previously, Vanburen's wife and five-month-old son had been evacuated from Singapore to Australia and he was able to locate them. A few months later he met some of his colleagues from the escape-run. Both he and they were now smartly dressed in RAAF uniform, having adjusted to their new situation.

5 Crossing Sumatra

Taken in stages over a distance approaching 300 miles, the route across Sumatra in 1942 must have seemed more akin to a voyage of exploration for Europeans who had lived in Singapore, and even to those who had spent many years in peninsular Malaya. For soldiers, sailors and airmen also it was very much new territory, offering a whole range of tropical scenery, some of it very dramatic. Travelling had to be done, however, as circumstances allowed; for many, this meant covering long distances at night.

From the coastal swamps and deltas along the Malacca Strait, the way inland lay along a broad, shallow river until the edge of the flood plain was reached. Here the first motor road began, rising with the land towards a north–south mountain range which rose in places to more than 12 000 feet. Twisting and turning sharply through the mountainous regions, the road through central Sumatra to the west coast reached a height of 3000 feet above the sea, before dropping sharply to the coastal area near Padang. From this height, too, a steep mountain railway ran down from Sawah Lunto in the centre of a coal-mining region, carrying passengers and freight to the fertile coastal plain below. Many who were transported by lorry over the mountains found it a hair-raising experience, though they praised the skill and calmness of the Asian drivers. Those fortunate enough to make the steep railway journey down by day recalled the great beauty and range of tropical scenery as they headed for the coast. On the long climb from the eastern side all had to cross the upper reaches of the Indragiri river by a ferry where flood-water could sometimes hold up road transport for days.

Along much of the route, population was sparse and the few riverside ports and market centres along the Indragiri were small and scattered. Only on the western side of Sumatra, between mountains and sea, was there extensive evidence of richer soils, village group-ings and plantation crops, such as rice, maize, groundnuts, sugar-cane, coffee and tobacco. Here and there, a rubber estate would appear, sometimes still in working use, sometimes obviously de-serted, its buildings showing signs of decay.

Occasionally, the house of a Dutch estate manager would be encountered but, typically, central Sumatra, and central-western Sumatra in particular, was the land of the Minangkabau Malays.

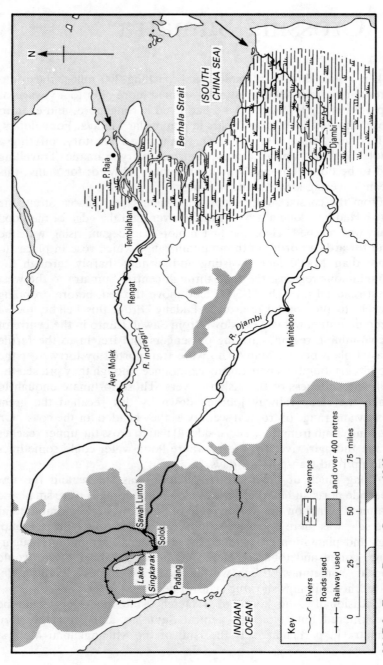

MAP 3 Escape Routes, Sumatra, 1942

Keen agriculturists with attractive villages and ancient cultural traditions, they were also alert and experienced traders. Few Chinese, or other non-Malay people, lived in this region outside the more European-influenced towns of Padang and Fort de Kock, the latter having been built originally as an early-nineteenth-century Dutch garrison township. Still a military base, Fort de Kock (Bukit Tinggi) was a Dutch administrative centre with a reputation among the Dutch as a health resort in the hills.

Few of the refugees from Singapore seem to have picked up much impression of Fort de Kock and its immediate neighbourhood. This appears to have been partly because the area was not specially selected as a staging point, and partly because of the amount of travelling done at night. One memoir did express regret at having missed much of the scenery in this area through night travel. 'The scenery must be quite unusually striking,' it read, 'such of the country as we saw in daylight was hilly and well cultivated with paddy fields.' For most soldiers and civilians who escaped from Singapore to Sumatra there were four or five main staging points across the island, but itineraries were not identical in all cases, as appears from the records of individuals and groups. Among the prominent places, however, were Rengat (the first main riverside port and market town on the Indragiri), a rubber estate at Ayer Molek, the plateau-based railhead at Sawah Lunto and, finally, the west-coast port of Padang and its environs.

In the late days at Singapore, a small group of military officers was organised to plan and assist in a limited military evacuation through Sumatra, a job which included leaving food dumps and instructions *en route*. Captain Ivan Lyon of the Gordon Highlanders was credited with having undertaken pioneer work on the route, Major 'Jock' Campbell (King's Own Scottish Borderers, and an ex-planter) was in charge during a critical period at Rengat, and Lieutenant-Colonel 'Andy' Dillon, former quarter-master general with the 18th Division sent to reinforce Malaya and Singapore, took charge at Ayer Molek. Colonel Alan Warren of the Royal Marines came to handle military movements at Padang, where there was also a resident British consul. Back at Tembilahan, at a fairly early stage of the route, Ernest Gordon, an Argylls captain, supervised the transit camp. In time, all these military officers were to move up the route themselves to reach Padang, but all except Campbell and Lyon were destined eventually to become prisoners of the Japanese.

Oswald Gilmour, Deputy Municipal Engineer at Singapore, managed to leave there on the *Kuala* on 13 February. Bombed and
shipwrecked with the Public Works Department contingent off Pom
Pong, he was picked up and able to reach Sumatra and the Indragiri
river. His journey across the island was subject to less restraints than
those of most of the military personnel, who felt the obligation to be
directed in companies or groups by senior officers, and who, for good
reason, did not want soldiers 'free-lancing' through Sumatra. Finding
a delay for organised transport at Ayer Molek, Mr Gilmour managed
to hire a car which took him and his companions as far as Tolek.
Here, they picked up further transport and chose to take a longer
route, via Pekan Baru, to avoid possible flood waters ahead. At
Pekan Baru, they were helped with money and car hire by a Dutch
'Controller' who was staying behind to hand over to the Japanese,
having sent his wife and child away first to Fort de Kock. The Dutch
officer was meanwhile supervising the carrying out of a 'scorched
earth' policy in his region, bewildered, as many of his fellow-
countrymen were, by the rapid fall of Singapore, and its consequences for Sumatra. At the time of the Japanese invasion of the Malay
Peninsula, people living in central Sumatra, both Asians and Europeans, must have seemed a long way, a safe distance surely, from the
war front. In a little over two months, the war had reached them.
Japanese troops were advancing northwards from Palembang and
already there were rumours of Japanese landings in the northern area
of Sumatra.

   Oswald Gilmour was among the lucky ones. He reached Padang,
admittedly to face uncertainty, but stayed with a Dutch family who
showed great kindness towards him, despite their own predicament.
A small freighter, the SS *Palopo*, from Java, called in at Emmahaven
for fuel and was rapidly coaled. It sailed early next morning, taking
Gilmour and about 50 others on board. There were still major risks.
The *Palopo* was a small vessel which could only reach about nine
knots. As they left port the day was cloudy and the dreaded Japanese
reconnaissance plane did not appear. (Gilmour, it must be recalled,
had met it all before, on the *Kuala* from Singapore.) Colonel Warren
at Padang had said the *Palopo* though small, might be the last ship to
call and there was no further information at the time. Threading
through the Siberut Strait at night, the *Palopo* slowly reached the open
sea and made for Ceylon. Three days out, they picked up two Malays
on a raft, survivors from a torpedoed evacuee ship from Padang. 'We
were,' wrote Gilmour, 'very, very lucky', recalling that they crossed

1. Jungle setting, Malaya, 1941

2. (*above*) Gurkhas with trench mortars, Malaya, 1941

3. (*below*) Malayan soldier in swamp country, Malaya, 1941

4. (*above*) British troops in bren-carriers, Malaya, 1941

5. (*below*) Burnt-out British Army vehicles which had been left to block the road and delay the Japanese advance near Senggarang, Johore, January 1942 (a Japanese photograph taken after the road had been cleared)

6. (*above*) HMS *Scout*

7. (*below*) HMS *Tenedos*

British destroyers which assisted at Padang

8. (*above*) HMS *Dragon*

9. (*below*) HMS *Danae*

innes photo press D.

British light cruisers which assisted at Padang

10. (*above*) HMAS *Hobart*. Australian cruiser engaged in rescue work at Padang

11. (*below*) HMS *Jupiter*. British destroyer active in evacuation from Singapore

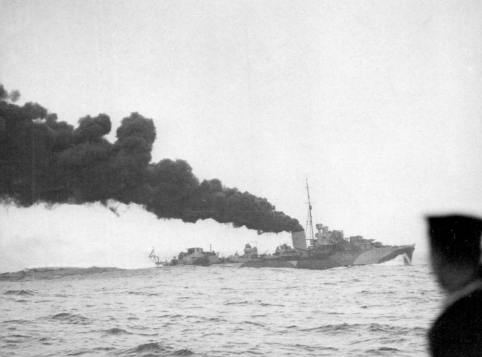

12. (*above*) Trooping ships arriving at Singapore, January 1942

13. (*below*) *Talthybius*, Blue Funnel cargo-liner, 1937

14. (*above*) Malay sailing vessel, *Sederhana Djohanis*, which crossed the Indian Ocean from West Sumatra

15. (*below*) Blue Funnel cargo-passenger ship, *Gorgon*, took civilian evacuees from Singapore to Fremantle, Australia

16. (*above*) and 17 (*below*): The waterfront of Singapore in flames and ships bombed at the docks (C. Yates McDaniel, Associated Press photograph taken 12 February 1942)

18. Captain (later Major) Desmond (Dudley) Apthorp, MBE, Royal Norfolk Regiment

19. Captain (later Major) W. S. P. B. ('Paddy') Martin, RIE

20. Cpl (later Sgt) Bob Tall, Royal Engineers

21. Sgt-Major (later Major) E. C. Hosking, RAOC

22. Lieutenant (later Captain) A. W. Nock, Royal Norfolk Regiment

23. Major J. W. P. Marsh, RAOC

24. Volunteers Captain George Patterson in 1946

the Indian Ocean, slowly, but safely. Retrospectively, he calculated that only a small number of those who left Singapore when he did made a successful departure from Padang. He was referring in particular to those who had originally sailed on the few ships he knew most about and estimated that, from these, perhaps 130 out of 1000 evacuees had managed to reach Padang and cross the Indian Ocean safely.

———————

Major Leech and his escape party (see Chapter 4) had left Singapore a day later than Oswald Gilmour and, after threading through the islands and up the Indragiri river, reached Tembilahan shortly after dawn on 24 February. As they recalled, it was a small village with a Dutch District Officer, a hospital and a barracks with a platoon of local troops. There was wireless communication with Rengat, up-river, and about 100 British troops from Singapore were waiting there. 'A Captain in a Highland Regiment' was in charge of the movement up to Rengat. Neither boats nor petrol or paraffin were available and it appeared that a number of launches had gone upstream and not been sent back. A delay of at least a day or two seemed likely until Major Leech and a Captain Beamish persuaded the Dutch officer to allow them to board an old launch going up to Rengat with local people and government stores.

The launch was dirty and overcrowded and the engine 'obviously on its last legs'. An hour after departure, the engine stopped. Two of the soldiers eventually got it going again by midnight and they anchored at a small village until next morning. In nine hours, they had travelled 28 miles and they were still a long way from Rengat. As they headed up the river again next morning, they noticed it was still about a quarter of a mile wide, with clumps of pale blue water hyacinth drifting by and sometimes colouring a whole stretch of water. Others noticed that this feature of the river, while attractive, could also be a hazard to slow-moving river craft.

During the morning of 25 February, there was another delay through engine failure and the same problem arose again in mid-afternoon as they tied up at a riverside quay at Kuala Tenaku. Fortunately, they had reached a point where a recent extension of the road from the west came down to the river, and from where it was

possible to telephone to the District Office in Rengat, which Major
Leech did, with a request for a lorry. A few hours later, the party of
14 was on its way by road to Rengat, and from there, at once,
directed onwards to the rubber estate at Ayer Molek. Here they
found about 170 troops from Singapore, with a Lieutenant-Colonel
Dillon as the senior officer in charge. Food was short and the
mosquitoes were hungry too, as the men tried to sleep on the wooden
benches of a rubber storehouse. When the rubber sheets were used as
overnight blankets, men were often found sticking to them next
morning. Despite the problems, things seem to have been well
organised at Ayer Molek. As the numbers rose, groups of both the
soldiers and the civilians who were here were put into order of
priority to await transport by lorry. But many waited several days,
numbers grew and tensions increased. Only about 40 people reportedly left Ayer Molek on 26 February, but Major Leech's group was
on the move the next day, half the party by lorry in the morning and
the other half by bus that afternoon. The lorry broke down after a
few miles and was helped later by the arrival of the bus with Leech,
who had taken a lift back to look for spare parts. There were
problems, too, about petrol, which they eventually obtained at
Tolek. By the end of the day they had crossed the Indragiri by ferry
and were drinking coffee in a small village.

Here it was learned that a train was expected to leave Sawah Lunto
for Padang at 1 a.m. next morning. They were in the mountainous
area and it rained heavily as the lorry driver drove at speed on the
twisting road, which often had a sheer drop on either side. The lorry
was open and the passengers were cold, utterly drenched and rather
bumped and bruised. It was 3 a.m. when they drove into the station
yard at Sawah Lunto and the train did not leave until more than an
hour later. In the meantime, the bus which had followed, at a more
cautious speed, with the other half of the party, arrived in time for its
passengers to transfer to rail transport, which, for most of those
involved, marked the last stage of their cross-Sumatran journey.
Padang was reached seven hours later.

By this time, some 700 civilians and service people were billeted in
Padang. In leadership roles were Colonel Warren of the Marines and
Mr Levinson, the resident British Consul. In the billeting arrangements, civilians and military were separated and, within the services,
officers and other ranks were also generally allocated to separate
quarters. For escapers and evacuees who had travelled from Singapore, Padang was easily the largest and most developed town they

had met, but they were naturally keen to leave it as quickly as possible. Only the sea now offered a way ahead.

An account by Lieutenant-Colonel B. H. Ashmore, an officer at Malayan Command, has provided one of the most detailed descriptions of the journey of a military party from Singapore to Sumatra, and across the island from east to west. This official evacuation group, consisting of ten officers and 100 other ranks, left Singapore on a minesweeper, HMS *Malacca*, during the late evening of 13 February. Early next morning they anchored by a small island to hide from air attacks during the day, and were joined there by a small steamer, packed with troops, and a water-boat. Nine Japanese bombers came over and attacked, but there were no casualties and there was little damage to the vessels. Many of the men were hidden on the island during the day and others took to boats after the bombing; this may have given the attackers a greater impression of success than had been achieved.

By late afternoon, *Malacca* was sailing again for Batavia, as the Malaya Command party was due to join up with South Western Pacific Command in Java. A broken pipe in the engine had been the only significant damage, and this was quickly repaired. As they sailed through the night it became apparent that many ships had been attacked and had suffered badly. Sometimes they were surrounded by people screaming and shouting in the water; these they tried to pick up. Eventually, in conference with the ship's captain, it was decided that it would be 'bitter madness' to try to make Batavia by way of the Bangka Strait, so the *Malacca*'s direction was changed, to head for the Sumatran coast. By skilful navigation, they entered the Indragiri river at 10 a.m. next morning and, with the further assistance of a river pilot taken on board, safely reached Tembilahan six hours later. The river was wide with a deep channel, and the jungle came down to the water's edge. Already, a large number of troops from Singapore was said to have arrived there, including wounded from the sunken ships.

The Dutch authorities found accommodation for the military party from the ship, and wounded, among whom there were some very bad cases, were placed in the local hospital. On the next morning, 16 February, some 300 other ranks and 20 officers headed up-river on the *Han Ann*, formerly the yacht of the Sultan of Kelantan; they reached Rengat in the late afternoon. Colonel Ashmore was full of praise for the Dutch arrangements to accommodate and feed the men, and a large party, increased to more than 400 in two river barges, was towed by launch up to the Ford rubber factory at Ayer Molek next day. These were lengthy, tedious and uncomfortable journeys and the tow broke twice on this day, but they were on the move, at the same time leaving space behind them for other parties to come through the staging points. At Rengat, and particularly at Ayer Molek, the numbers were growing quickly and they included sailors, RAF men and Australian troops. Early on 18 February, a fleet of motor-buses had assembled at the rubber factory and a long convoy took off by road for Sawah Lunto. It was an all-day journey 'through wonderful country' and when local people were seen, they were friendly and helpful. After a short rest and a meal at Sawah Lunto, by which time another party of 200 had arrived, all were settled on a night train for Padang, where they arrived at 7 a.m. next morning, 19 February. Here they were accommodated in the Malay school, with a few senior officers sharing rooms, and the floor, at the Central Hotel. Lieutenant-Colonel G. A. Palmer RE, from Malaya Command, was already in Padang and had made arrangements with the Dutch ahead of the main party; this was a role to be taken over a few days later by Colonel Alan Warren of the Royal Marines.

A cable message to headquarters in Java resulted in HMS *Danae* arriving at Emmahaven on the evening of 21 February and taking off 80 officers and 550 other ranks, and disembarking them at Tjiliatjap, in southern Java, two days later. From there, they travelled by train to a camp setting some 25 miles inland. Within days, however, it was clear that, in the wake of Japanese successes in western Java, the Allies were going to pull out of the island. Another sea-voyage would be in prospect.

What seems to emerge most from Colonel Ashmore's account is the extraordinary smoothness of the arrangements for conveying large numbers of displaced troops across Sumatra, given the difficult terrain and the various forms of transport necessary. This was all the more impressive in an operation which, in the nature of things, could not have had long planning behind it. These particular groups arrived in Sumatra less than a day after the fall of Singapore and reached the west coast of the island three days later. For the next three weeks or so, military and civilian groups from Singapore were still arriving in Padang and it was obviously not surprising if the organisation 'creaked' at times, particularly in the maintenance of a flow of transport to and from some of the key places *en route*. It was perhaps less remarkable that there were hold-ups and delays at times, than that the 'system', with whatever shortcomings it developed, at least continued in operation as long as it did.

Alex Niven, of the Public Works Department in Malaya, was one of a boat party which reached Perigi Raja, near the estuary of the Indragiri, only to find the place deserted, so they continued up to Tembilahan. Here they were told they should stay the night and continue their journey next morning. Two godowns near the water's edge had been put at the disposal of people passing through, and a hot meal was prepared at the school-house. Niven and some of his companions found two concrete water tanks full of water and 'proceeded to luxuriate in a dipper bath', the first bath they had managed for eight days. When they had stepped off the boat, he thought they must have looked like 'some collection of freaks from a circus sideshow'.

About the same time, Mr W. F. Wegener of the Federated Malay States Railways reached Tembilahan, and his official report later referred to the evacuation organisation which he met here. He had a good meal and Straits money was changed for Dutch currency before his party moved up-river by barge; perhaps this was the nearest the journey came to tourism. But there followed a bad night and day on the barge, 'with periods of alternating intense heat and violent rainstorms'. Next day, he found an 'improvised evacuation service' at Rengat, with Major Campbell in charge. A meal was provided and the night was spent in a disused godown near the river front.

On Friday 27 February, Wegener was in a small party of about 14 which left Rengat by motor bus, with a Lieutenant Scott in charge. They were driven some 30 miles to the rubber estate at Ayer Molek, where they found 'a large concentration of services personnel waiting to leave for Padang'; estimates ranged from 600 to 1000. Parties continued to leave by bus during the day. Wegener's own group was not unduly delayed, as they left next morning by bus for the railhead at Sawah Lunto, stopping on the way at Tolek, where they saw Dr Jean Lyon, of the Malayan Medical Services, nursing some severely wounded who were unfit to travel further. At Sawah Lunto also, a woman doctor, Dr Ethel Morris, was similarly engaged, looking after the sick and wounded. Earlier, at Tembilahan, a woman was in hospital with a leg blown off and in a gangrenous state.

On the evening of Sunday 1 March, Mr. Wegener's group continued their journey by train, arriving at Padang at 1.15 a.m. next morning. Whether the railway engineer found this section exciting is not, apparently, on record; like many others, he followed it during the hours of darkness. At Padang, accommodation and food were found in a school building which was already said to be holding about 200 Australian troops. (Both a Malay and a Chinese school were in use at the time.) But the timing was fortunate. That evening, all who were in the school, troops and civilians, marched back to the railway station and entrained for the docks at Emmahaven, where a Dutch steamer, the *De Veert*, was waiting. They sailed at 2 a.m. on Tuesday 3 March, and made a safe crossing of the Indian Ocean to Colombo, where they arrived on 9 March. It was a slow crossing and both food and water on board were scarce. The passengers were, no doubt, uncomfortably crowded, but they had reason to be thankful. Only five days ahead of them, and well on the way to Colombo, a Dutch ship, the *Rooseboom* had been torpedoed with a heavy loss of lives, many suffering a lingering and terrifying death in the one overloaded lifeboat which drifted helplessly away. Time was now running out at Emmahaven. From the coastline near Padang only the attempts of small groups to challenge the Indian Ocean in Malay sailing boats were recorded after 6 March.

It was not surprising that some of the more enterprising 'escapers' felt frustrated by delays on their passage through Sumatra. Paddy Martin recorded later, 'we had many delays after reaching Rengat and I think they were the things that nearly got us down; arrangements had to be hurriedly made and, more often than not, were inefficient, so that we got eternally held up'. Although he was very tired and his legs were badly swollen, he found a waiting period of two days in a crepe-drying shed at Ayer Molek very tedious. An Engineers' captain, 'Mike' Jennings, who had made a late escape from Singapore, found Ayer Molek well organised under Colonel Dillon, who arranged a sequence of numbered parties under appointed leaders. Jennings himself was put in charge of 'party No.14', a military group made up mostly of sappers and anti-tank personnel. At this stage, the numbers of military and civilians waiting at Ayer Molek still ran into several hundreds and they included women and children. There were long delays on a waiting list for road transport and, after five days, Jennings and his party decided to walk to the next staging post, 100 miles ahead at Tolek. On the way, they were hospitably received by the manager of a Dutch-owned rubber estate, but, by the third day, lorries from Ayer Molek had begun to overtake them, first with British women, then with men from the services. A Dutch army sergeant gave them a lift in his lorry but, at Tolek, they were once again caught up in the organised arrangements and placed at the back of the queue. They spent a full week at Tolek before moving off again on 8 March, by which time, had they known it, the last possible rescue ship had already left Padang. They eventually completed the journey by road to Sawah Lunto and from there by mountain railway to Padang, where Jennings was in time to join other officers to hear a 'pep talk' from Colonel Warren, during which a possible hope of rescue by the navy was expressed. Three naval cruisers, two British and one Australian, and two British destroyers had called at Padang and taken off quite a large number of people on 1 March, but it needed more optimism than Jennings could muster to think this type of operation would happen a second time. He began to think in terms of organising a small boat party.

Earlier, the soldiers with Major Leech who had reached Padang on 28 February found prospects of a rescue 'more than doubtful', the only hope seemed to be that 'a Dutch trading vessel might call in sometime, when – nobody knows'. They estimated that there were 700 'British' people in the town, including civilians and members of the Malayan Public Works Department, Queen Alexandra nurses, Australians and 'Chinese irregulars'. Plans for the local defence of Padang were under discussion.

The next day began with no better news. There were stories of Japanese landings in Java and further advances in Sumatra, where Japanese troops were believed to have reached Rengat. Studying a map on the schoolroom wall where they were staying, Leech's party began to consider the possibility of finding and provisioning a small boat. At 4 p.m. that afternoon, a British naval warship lay off Padang and 400 troops were quickly marshalled down to the port, to be taken off to Colombo. Major Leech and his companions were not among them and they began to resign themselves to the task of holding part of the perimeter of Padang against a pending Japanese attack. Leech was to command a fighting company of about half of the available troops and Beamish, his 'No.2', was to be Defence and Security Officer, engaged in reconnaissance work in liaison with a Dutch commander.

These preliminary decisions had scarcely been reached when news was received that there were no less than five British warships at the port and that they would take off all 'British' groups stranded in the town. Within an hour or two, Leech's party and the rest had travelled by train down to the harbour, boarded a destroyer and been transferred to a cruiser. That night, they began the crossing of the Indian Ocean. Except for Major Leech himself, who had left France a few days earlier, the Northumberland Fusiliers in his group had all been evacuated from Dunkirk by the Royal Navy in 1940. Padang was the second time the 'senior service' had come to their assistance.

In the event, nothing could have been done to save Padang from the Japanese and, realising this, the local Dutch authorities declared it an 'open' town. Senior Dutch officials and the British Consul and his wife awaited the arrival of the Japanese but, all the time, other evacuees and escapers were still arriving and two Dutch cargo ships carried many away, some to Java and some to Ceylon. In the official record of these events, the two destroyers and three cruisers had called at Emmahaven in search of fuel and they carried away to safety some 800 military personnel and civilians. All the time, others were arriving to fill up the emergency accommodation in Padang. The harbour at Emmahaven was bombed more than once and no one could assess the extent of the dangers to shipping which moved from the western Sumatran coast. It was rumoured, with later justification, that Japanese submarines were operating in the Indian Ocean.

After 6 March, no further merchant or naval ships appear to have put in at Emmahaven. Charles Samuel, a Penang lawyer, who arrived at Padang on 7 March recorded in his diary, 'we were all waiting expectantly for a boat from Colombo to arrive and take us away, but none came'. The days passed, as he put it, 'tediously', until 16 March, when local police made it known that the first Japanese troops could be expected in the town next day; this message proved to be correct and it was a chilling end of journey for so many who had started out from Singapore a month earlier and had survived so much danger and hardship on the way.

More than a week earlier, Colonel Warren of the Marines had quietly selected volunteers to attempt escape from Sumatra in a traditional Malay prahu, or sailing boat. Three other notable attempts to escape by sea followed. Naval Reserve Officer

Cunyngham-Brown had been engaged on several rescue missions round the islands in the archipelago, but had reached Padang too late. With the support of Colonel Warren, he set about finding boats along the coast to take himself and a party of officers to freedom, across the Indian Ocean. There was also an escape attempt by Colonel Dillon, who had helped to run the escape organisation across Sumatra, especially at Ayer Molek. Eventually, he reached Padang, too, and, as related later, embarked on another extremely hazardous small boat project from the Sumatran coast. Captain 'Mike' Jennings of the Royal Engineers had still been well inland when the last rescue ship left from Emmahaven. Whether it was 'the last' was not, of course, clear at the time, but by the time Jennings reached Padang he had little faith in the prospect of more shipping, and sought means of trying to help himself and any small group which would venture with him. Like the other attempts, it would be something of a desperate last gamble and its course is summarised in a later chapter.

Meanwhile, there is more to relate about those who crossed Sumatra, and also about the situation of those who were left behind at Padang. There was an alternative to the Indragiri River route for much of the journey across Sumatra and this was used by Peter Cardew, an engineer of the Public Works Department in Malaya, and his 12 companions, who reached the estuary of the Djambi (Hari) river in a small boat from the island of Singkep. In his own account, Cardew recorded that they had 'turned up this river' with the intention of reaching Padang on the west coast. That morning, he went down with malaria and the next five or six days which it took to reach the coast proved something of a nightmare for him. At Djambi, 100 miles or so upstream, they transferred, somewhat reluctantly, to a Dutch launch which was even smaller than their own boat, but which was claimed to be more suited to the shallow river from this point onwards. The launch soon broke down and they negotiated for the hire of a Chinese bus, which only managed a further 20 miles along the road, and then a Dutch military convoy picked them up and took them to the town of Mariteboe. Other British evacuees and escapers were already in the town, where the local Dutch administration looked after them, providing buses and lorries in which they proceeded in convoy towards Padang. By noon next day they had reached Sawah Lunto in the mountains, where they were given a hot meal. At 5 a.m. on the following morning they were 'shoved on a train' to Padang. Although Peter Cardew's memory was blurred by the intermittent bouts of malaria from which he was suffering, it is evident from this account that his party moved on quickly and, despite some incidental difficulties, was well looked after on the way.

Lieutenant W. J. B. Johnson, of the Royal Naval Reserve, also reached the Sumatran coast near the estuary of the Djambi river after an overnight motorboat voyage from Singkep and 'a very tricky two hours' off a lee shore, with the sea 'dead slow'. Eventually, they entered the river and proceeded as far as the town of Djambi, where they abandoned their boat and were picked up by a Dutch military convoy and taken to Mariteboe. The Dutch soldiers were armed with Italian rifles captured in Libya and expected to encounter Japanese troops at any time along the road. There was, apparently, little or no waiting along this route, as Johnson and his party continued, according to his account, to 'a place called Solok', and then by train to Padang. By this time a cut in Johnson's leg had 'gone thoroughly septic' and he was admitted to the local hospital with a very high temperature.

Solok lay south and west of Sawah Lunto and, for those who used it, the Djambi–Mariteboe–Solok route appears to have worked well. It was not facing the same challenge of numbers experienced further north along the Indragiri route and, consequently, was less liable to the kind of bottleneck which could occur at Ayer Molek, or Tolek, while road transport was awaited. Lieutenant Johnsons's travels in Sumatra, however, were far from over. On his second day in hospital, his party arrived to tell him that a ship was leaving for Java that night, would he be able to make it? Despite his continuing high temperature of 105°, he left the hospital and was soon carried aboard a Dutch coastal steamer. There were no medical arrangements on board, he could not eat the boiled rice and corned beef which was the staple food on the ship and, with the condition of his leg steadily worsening, he felt in danger of his life.

In the end, he pleaded to be put ashore at a place named Endraboera down the Sumatran coast, where contact was being made with an agent of the shipping company. Lowered into a small boat, he was taken ashore by the agent who took him to his own house. There he was given the kindest of nursing attention by a Malay wife, while a message went to the Dutch District Officer, who, in turn, sent transport to have Johnson brought up to his residence, three hours' drive away. Finally, after more food and rest, there followed another journey to a hospital 4500 feet up in the mountains, on a large tea estate at Kaju Aro in west central Sumatra.

By this time, the naval officer's temperature was up to 106° or 107°. Virtually all the hospital staff was engaged to look after him and it was decided to operate on his leg at once in order to remove gangrenous matter. Two stiff whiskies had to serve in the absence of any anaesthetics. Johnson had reached a 'beyond caring' point, but under constant attention, his temperature went down and his leg was patched up. He heard that the Japanese were just the other side of the mountain and wanted to be away again, with perhaps a last chance to escape. Fitted out with clothing and money and put on a truck, he was driven for 12 hours to Padang, possibly the only escaper to come away from that town and return to try again. After 24 hours in the hospital once more, he heard there was a British cruiser calling at the port and managed to be on the spot again. This time, thanks to the Royal Navy, he was bound for Colombo, a further period of recuperation and a spell of sick leave. He acknowledged an immense debt of gratitude to all who had helped him.

———————

Among the many people who were rescued by the British navy at Padang was Martin Ogle, formerly in the Education service in Penang. His recollections of travelling along the main escape route in Sumatra tended to emphasise the orderliness of arrangements. Referring, first, to the use of buses from one emergency camp to another, he also noted the rota system, whereby people travelled on according to their individual arrival times and periods of waiting; he found this system also operating for the trains from Sawah Lunto to Padang, where he arrived on or about 28 February. Lists were drawn up here of both civilian and military personnel, the military being expected to have the first chance of leaving, together with any women and children evacuees. When the British Consul took down the names of civilians, Ogle, and some others with him who had experienced only 10 weeks of part-time military training after joining the Volunteers, felt they were more 'civilians' than 'military' and forfeited any possible claims to priority. Although, from other evidence, it is clear that Martin Ogle served conscientiously with the Volunteers, he had consistently felt that British officers in government service in Malaya could have been more effectively used during the Malayan Campaign in duties pertaining to civil administration or liaison work with the military, rather than becoming hastily prepared soldiers, willy-nilly.

As and when a ship came in, people were to be 'named' according to their place on one of the lists and everyone was advised to take the first ship on offer; there might not be another. As the word got quickly round Padang on 1 March that 'the navy's here', there was a rush down to the railway station, using any transport that was to hand. An allocation of civilian places for departure consisted of 69 names and Ogle and some of his companions were placed in the 70s in the list, but not everyone in the first 70 appeared and they were allowed through to fill up the places. Martin Ogle's own estimate that 500 to 600 people were taken off at the time was lower than the later 'official' figure of approximately 800, but there seems no question that these departures were generally well organised and orderly. Given all the circumstances, this was remarkable enough. The cruisers were HMS *Danae*, HMS *Dragon* and HMAS *Hobart*; Martin Ogle was transferred to the last-named vessel, which reached Colombo safely on 5 March. Also departing with HMAS *Hobart* was Mr T. G Husband, a senior man among the Public Works Department people who had originally left Singapore on the *Kuala*, and been bombed and shipwrecked at Pom Pong. He recalled later having embarked on a destroyer which raced out to the cruiser and then scrambling up the sides of the ship by rope-ladder. There was great urgency about the whole operation and they had a fast and uneventful 'trip' across to Colombo. From there, he sailed on to Bombay, where the Public Works people evacuated from Malaya were assembled and transferred to jobs in various parts of the Empire. This took about six weeks and then Mr Husband was allowed sick leave to join his family who had earlier reached Australia.

The handling of a large number of soldiers and others in transit at Padang must have been a delicate and difficult task, and a great deal of responsibility for it was taken by the Marines Colonel, Alan Warren, who had earlier been a member of a Special Operations Unit based on Singapore. Arriving at Padang on 24 February, Warren found himself more or less taking charge straight away on the military side, after a brigadier had gone through and the Australian general had quickly flown out. While orderly arrangements were maintained for movements to the docks, there were reported incidents of disgraceful behaviour by British and Australian troops in town, which incurred the anger of the local Dutch Military Commander and hostility from the resident Dutch in the local population. As the prospects of movement away from Padang began to recede, Warren was doing his best to maintain military discipline and to offer military co-operation with the Dutch, particularly for a guerilla-type resistance against the Japanese. He was also discreetly selecting men for an escape party in a traditional Malay boat and making it known that he would assist any reasonable escape plan that was brought before him.

Among those whom Warren met in connection with possible escapes was RN Reserve officer Cunyngham-Brown who, on the *Hung Jao*, had been actively helping evacuees on the Singapore–Sumatra route ever since the fall of Singapore. When he arrived at Padang too late for merchant ships or the navy, Cunyngham-Brown was given help and encouragement by Warren to search along the coast for local Malay craft with a view to getting a party of former staff officers from Malayan Command away to Ceylon.

A Dutch decision to declare Padang 'open' put an end to any thoughts or plans of organised late resistance to the Japanese, from whom an advance party arrived in the area on 17 March. Colonel Warren joined the Dutch civil Governor and the British Consul in a meeting with the Japanese to settle surrender details. He had deliberately chosen not to seek his own freedom and was to spend the next $3\frac{1}{2}$ years in captivity, which were to include a long period on the notorious Burma–Siam railway. Several hundred British and Allied troops were still in Padang, perhaps as many as half the total of those who had managed to leave, though not all successfully. At least four serious attempts were being made to tackle ocean routes with small Malay craft.

Among those 'caught' at Padang were many civilians, whose numbers included the British Consul and his wife and British expatriates from Malaya and Singapore. Charles Samuel, a Penang lawyer of long standing in Malaya, wrote in his diary: 'On 17 March, the Japanese arrived and soon visited us, removing the beds and mattresses and any personal belongings, including razor, cigarette-case, towel.' He had become an internee, an 'enemy alien'. On Samuel's record, there were 55 British male civilians as well as the British

Consul, whose wife was held with other women, British and Dutch. Most of the accounts of the journey across Sumatra and what followed from it have come from men, both soldiers and civilians, though women not infrequently kept diaries in internment camps. The few accounts by women do help to fill a useful gap, and provide a different viewpoint.

Miss Edith Wood (as she was) was a nursing sister among those bombed and shipwrecked on the *Kuala* and she subsequently worked with the seriously ill and wounded as they made their way through the island, first to Singkep and then to eastern Sumatra. Edith had survived, first on a raft, then in a sampan, as she crossed from island to island. At Singkep, she 'came out of the hat' as a volunteer to accompany sick and wounded patients on the converted hospital ship, *Heather*, normally a Singapore water-tanker. On the morning of 25 February, Nurse Wood and another nurse, Muriel Bostock, were able to leave their immediate patients at Tanjong Djabung on the Indragiri, from where they were driven in a van by a Dutch soldier returning to his unit at Kluang. After further help from a Dutch family, the two nurses were on the road again by lorry, to reach Sawah Lunto on the evening of the 26th. From there, a British army medical officer, Major Davis, arranged for them to be on the train next day and to be met and looked after at the Endraacht Club in Padang, on arrival there. They did not have to wait long. It transpired that there was a Dutch cargo vessel due to leave for Batavia that night and they were asked whether they would care to risk another sea voyage. They agreed to this offer and soon found themselves tending the sick and wounded on a vessel with no ship's doctor, carrying away 200 servicemen who had escaped from Singapore.

The ship was provisioned for the crew only and for six days; in the event, it was a ten-day voyage and both the crew and the passengers had to be fed from very meagre supplies. On the way out from Emmahaven, the captain heard that Java had fallen to the Japanese, premature news as it turned out, but certainly there was no safe approach to Java around that time, 1 March. A change of course was ordered and they headed instead for Colombo, arriving safely on or about 6 March. As was often the case in these emergencies, the captain was far from familiar with the sea-route; he was said to have been helped by a submarine commander on board.

By contrast, another *Kuala* victim and nurse, Mrs M. de Malmanche, arrived at Padang too late for any rescue ship and was interned in Sumatra for $3\frac{1}{2}$ years. Ironically, her husband, who was on duty in Singapore when she left there, reached India. During her journey across Sumatra, she was very much occupied with looking after the sick and wounded. At Rengat, she worked in the hospital until some small buses and ambulances were arranged for a party of sick and wounded and accompanying doctors and nurses; she travelled with this convoy to Tolek, staying there for a week. Fresh convoys of patients were arriving there every afternoon. One morning, one of the bus drivers said their's would be the last convoy and no more patients would be coming through. Mrs Malmanche therefore decided to join one of the buses going through to Sawah Lunto, keeping in the company of another nurse and two women doctors. At Sawah Lunto, they were met by RAMC Major Davis, who judged that Dr Crowe, one of the two women doctors, was too ill to continue; the other doctor, Dr Lyon, volunteered to stay with her and the two nurses were instructed to proceed to Padang by train early next morning.

Mrs Malmanche recalled the train journey as having passed through magnificent mountain country, where huge trees stood out on thickly wooded slopes. They skirted the great lake of Singora, then rolled into Padang Panjong and, 20 minutes later, the town of Padang. Here they were met by 'a most immaculate-looking officer', who introduced himself as Colonel Warren of the Royal Marines; with him was 'an equally spruce' naval officer, his aide, Captain Lind. Soon, the two nurses were helped to settle at the Dutch Social Club, but there many sick and wounded in need of attention and ten nurses were kept busy dealing with these cases for several hours each day. When Japanese entry into the town of Padang was imminent, Colonel Warren sent the two women doctors (now both in Padang) and all the nurses to a small Salvation Army hospital, run by a matron, Mrs Mepham, and her husband, both Canadians. The Colonel hoped the women would be safer there.

Mrs Malmanche recorded the presence of about 40 British women internees at Padang as well as 2500 women in the Dutch camp. There was also a large convent population, which included nuns and orphan children, sharing a complex of church, convent and school, with overcrowding everywhere. In 1943, all these internees were moved by train and truck to another campsite at Bangkinang in central Sumatra. In the diary kept by Charles Samuel, 500 male Dutch internees were noted at Padang just after the Japanese had taken control there. Many of the Dutch men were on military service and became prisoners-of-war.

While Padang had been the point of departure for some, it had
been the terminus for others. A point of departure was not, in any
case, a point of safe departure and, of the many who passed through,
some went on only to perish in the open sea, or later prison camp.
The journey across Sumatra had been long and arduous and, as a
route to freedom, it had still not always been enough.

6 The Role of the Dutch

British and Allied soldiers and civilians who escaped, or were evacuated, from Singapore, heading in a southerly direction, relied heavily on goodwill and co-operation in the Netherlands East Indies. Their passage was commonly through the island world of the Malay Archipelago to Sumatra or Java, to be followed, where possible, by long sea-voyages from Sumatra or Javanese ports. In 1941, all this was Dutch colonial territory, but it was an area in which the first Japanese attacks were being made at about the time of the fall of Singapore; further east, Dutch territory had been invaded earlier.

In September 1940, a Japanese delegation had visited Java to seek Dutch co-operation in a Japanese 'co-prosperity plan'. The Japanese government hoped at the time that Britain would capitulate to Germany and the Dutch would be persuaded to accept a Japanese 'protectorate' over their Indonesian empire. It was very much the same tactic which was used in relation to the French territories in Indo-China, enabling the Japanese to advance their interests and strategic positions without having to fight for the advantage gained. Britain did not fall and the Dutch refused to 'co-operate'. To that extent, Britain's successful defensive role in 1940, following the German conquest of France, Holland and Belgium, provided a shield for the Dutch in the East, and the immediate Japanese threat receded.

In the pattern of events, it was only a matter of time before the Japanese came to seize by military means what they had failed to achieve by aggressive diplomacy. Oil and other vital raw materials produced in the Netherlands East Indies were part of the attraction; the destruction of another Western empire and its replacement by new Asian states necessarily looking to Japan for leadership was the other part of the vision.

Starting with a chartered trading company at the beginning of the seventeenth century, the Dutch had built up their empire in South-East Asia through a mixture of trade and political treaties, and the spasmodic use of sea and land forces. Early on, they had ousted first the Portuguese and then the British from the vicinity of Java and the Malacca Straits. During the Napoleonic Wars, another period when the Netherlands lay under foreign domination, Britain gained temporary supremacy in Java, but, by the Treaty of London in 1824,

Britain and Holland agreed a delineation of spheres of interest. By this arrangement, the English East India Company, with a new base at Singapore, gained freedom of action from the Dutch in Singapore and the Malay Peninsula while undertaking not to interfere in Dutch activities further south. While this treaty left the way open for some later controversy about parts of North Borneo, it did generally serve its purpose of keeping the peace between two Western colonial powers. It pointed the way towards a 'British' Malaya and a 'Netherlands' East Indies.

In their colonial policies, the Dutch were often very enterprising and very energetic. They applied both capital and technical skills to develop the resources of their vast empire, which became one of the world's greatest producers and exporters of primary products. Increased food production and improving standards of health and hygiene fostered population growth and new areas of agricultural and industrial development were opened up. Yet there were political weaknesses in the Dutch system. Well into the twentieth century, for instance, the Dutch were engaged in a long and costly struggle with the people of northern Sumatra, and nationalist movements were evident elsewhere. Despite evidence of opposition to Dutch rule their administrative system was impressive, with its mixture of direct and less-direct government, and its system of administrative districts under the supervision of '*Controlleurs*'. The help and co-operation of these district officers was often vital to British and Allied soldiers and civilians using escape routes through Dutch territory in February and March 1942.

The colonial governments of the Netherlands East Indies did not respond quickly to pressures from Indonesian nationalist movements for devolution of political power, especially as there were divisions among the nationalists themselves. The conquest of Holland by Germany in 1940 was a severe blow to Dutch morale and prestige in the East and it added another dimension to the problem of security in their own colonial territory.

In the years just prior to the Japanese war, there were some 240 000 Europeans in the Netherlands East Indies, of whom more than 200 000 were counted as Dutch, that is Dutch and Dutch/ Eurasian. About three-quarters of the 'European' population lived in Java and most of the remainder in Sumatra. In earlier periods of Dutch rule in the Indies, 'mixed' marriages between Europeans and Asians had not been uncommon and many Eurasian families traced back over several generations. Legally, European Dutch Eurasians were on the same footing and counted as 'Dutch'. From about the beginning of the twentieth century, there was a proportionate increase in immigration from Europe, a reflection, in part, of rapidly improving communications. Whereas the British in Malaya constituted an essentially 'expatriate' community of people and families who 'came and went', about two-thirds of the 'legal' Dutch in the East Indies were Eurasians who had lived nowhere else, and the remaining one-third divided into those who were settlers (*'trekkers'*) and those who expected one day to return to their native land (*'hijvers'*).

Put in the simplest terms, the Dutch in the East Indies suffered, first, from the course of the European war and the loss of the contact with Holland from 1940, and then were faced by a Japanese invasion of their tropical island world which was to leave them completely defeated and dominated. Nor could they make any assumptions about the future, as the Japanese message of 'liberation', and 'Asia for the Asians' was in itself a welcome message to many Indonesians, though they had no real wish to see Japanese control replacing that of the Dutch. When, in the course of the Japanese military conquest and occupation of the Indies, guerilla groups began to form, there were clear signs that, whatever they stood for, it was not the status quo of the period up to February/March 1942. For the Dutch of the East Indies, the war in its widest setting was a doubly cruel event. Cut off from a European base, and facing the military and naval strength of Japan, they were also to find the internal unity of their territory being put to the test. Adding to the gloom of the situation was the dramatic failure of the British and their Allies in Malaya and Singapore, the hurried establishment of a new joint defence headquarers (ABDA) in Java and the quite unforeseen use of routes through their territories by escapers and evacuees from Singapore.

There can be no doubt that the Dutch were deeply shocked and upset by the news of the fall of Singapore. As early as 11 February 1942, a Dutch officer on a ship taking British women evacuees from Singapore to Batavia did not hide his feelings about the military weaknesses of the British and their behaviour in defeat. Nearly three weeks later, Dutch military officers at Padang in western Sumatra were asking Britons for reasons for their defeat at Singapore. This was hardly surprising, since it was a question the British would be asking themselves over and over again. If, as might well be expected, Dutch administrators and military officers felt 'let down' by what happened at Singapore, their attitude towards helping evacuees and escapers pass through Dutch territory does not appear to have been heavily influenced by the event. There was, on the contrary, a great deal of evidence of a generous spirit on the part of the Dutch, some of which could certainly be described as well beyond the call of duty. Some broader influences affected the situation. The overseas Dutch had admired Britain's stand against Hitler's Germany, following the fall of Holland, France and Belgium. British action in 1940 warded off unwelcome pressure by Japan in the Indies, and a 'Free Dutch' government resided in Britain. Many Dutch servicemen had escaped from the continent to continue to fight for the liberation of their country and the British had provided hospitality for Dutch civilian refugees. When British expatriate civilians from Malaya and Singapore began to arrive as refugees in Java and Sumatra there was evidence of ready sympathy on the part of the resident Dutch. Mrs Muriel Riley came from Singapore to Batavia with no money and virtually no luggage. A local hotelier found her a room and meals as long as she was able to stay. He insisted that he regarded this gesture as repaying, in a small way, a debt on behalf of his family; a niece of his had been warmly received and looked after when she arrived in England as a penniless refugee in 1940.

Dutch goodwill in the East Indies was certainly tested during the short period between the military campaign in Malaya and the Japanese conquest of the whole region. Until first Sumatra and then Java were attacked, some of the Dutch in the smaller islands to the south of Singapore were themselves able to seek refuge further south. Earlier still, there had been a small amount of movement of women and children to Australia and even the USA. But there was no widespread evacuation from the country; there were too many Dutch people and where could they go, or even be willing to go?

In general, the Dutch were willing enough to fight in the defence of their territory, but their resources were limited. The army of the Royal Netherlands Indies totalled about 40 000 troops, most of whom were Dutch and Eurasian. Traditionally, the function of this army had been to concern itself with matters of internal control, local or regional disturbances, insurrections, and the like, rather than to man defence positions against possible external attack. For this reason, and also because of the scattered and difficult nature of the settlement patterns, military units were often broken down into very small companies, useful for local patrol work, but insufficiently co-ordinated for any major operation. In terms of numbers, the army was mostly stationed in Java, where the great majority of the population lived. In addition to the regular, professional, troops, a militia force of Indonesians, about 7000 strong, had been recruited and, in the urban areas, there was a local defence organisation of 'town guards'. The total ground forces which could have been counted solely for the defence of Java would hardly have exceeded 40 000, and a very mixed company at that, including army and RAF remnants from Singapore, and a few Americans. The north coast of Java alone stretched for 700 miles, and the problems of defending it against an enemy with superior air and sea power were virtually insuperable. The fact that there was no larger 'territorial' army in Java, or elsewhere in the Indies, was at least partly due to the dangers inherent in arming a large force within which there were uncertain loyalties. A smaller army could be more carefully recruited and the non-Europeans traditionally came from particular regions of the Indies.

When, at the turn of the year 1942, the ABDA (American, British, Dutch Area) organisation was set up, the leading commands went to the Americans and the British and naval dispositions tended, at first, to emphasise a role of keeping open communications with Singapore, rather than preparing for the defence of the Indies. This was only in line with Britain's own policy of supplying reinforcements to Singapore when it might have been judged that the time for this was too late, and it could not have offered much comfort to the Dutch. After the fall of Singapore, the prospects for the Dutch in the East Indies were particularly bleak. Japanese troops arrived at Palembang in Sumatra on 17 February and were in general control of southern Sumatra within a few days. In the whole large island of Sumatra there were only some seven battalions of the Royal Netherlands Indies army and all Allied forces were evacuated hurriedly to Java. After sealing off the approaches to Java from both west and east, by local landings and the control of the main sea-passages, the Japanese began their main amphibious attacks from the Java Sea at the end of February. The ABDA command had by this date been dissolved and Dutch commanders were left to get on with the defence of their territory as best they could and without much Allied help. Many of the Dutch officers and men were fighting to defend the land in which they had been born and they knew that no reinforcements would now arrive. At sea, where the Dutch showed particular bravery, virtually all the Dutch naval vessels were sunk; while on land, the odds against the defenders were such that they could do little more than delay the final outcome. Major towns, their populations swollen by refugees, were declared 'open' as the Japanese forces approached.

The Dutch in Java surrendered to the Japanese on 8 March and a further surrender of Allied forces took place there on 12 March. Meanwhile, Japanese control of Sumatra had been gradually spreading; it reached the west coast port of Padang on 17 March and any remaining military operations centred chiefly on pockets of resistance and guerilla activities. Within little more than a month of their dramatic success at Singapore, the Japanese became the masters of the erstwhile Dutch colonial empire in the East Indies. Relationships between the East Indies Dutch and any British and Allied escapers or evacuees from Singapore whom they encountered can only be properly considered within the wider context of what was happening in the Indies at the time. That there were some clashes of opinion and divergencies of interest need be no matter for surprise; more noteworthy was the range of circumstances in which Dutch help and co-operation were still readily forthcoming.

In a report entitled 'Singapore to Colombo, 1942', Colonel Ashmore went out of his way to praise the support of the Dutch in Sumatra. 'The local Dutch authorities at Tembilahan', he wrote 'were splendid and did everything in their power to help'. At Rengat, the District Commissioner (Dutch) 'was tireless in his efforts to assist and make things comfortable for the wounded', and at Ayer Molek, 'excellent arrangements had been made by the Dutch army, the manager of the factory and his staff'. It was the same at Sawah Lunto, where 'the Dutch railway officials were excellent and fully out to help; they seemed most anxious to get as many men as possible to the west coast, and as quickly as possible'. Again, in Java, where he disembarked from HMS *Danae*, Colonel Ashmore noted that 'the Dutch had made excellent preparations in cooperation with the Movement Control staff of South West Pacific Command'. As the news came through, on 26 February, that the Allied HQ in Java was closing down, the Dutch and the Javanese 'were still extremely friendly and seemed resigned to the future', but 'some of the Dutch officers gave the impression that they thought we were abandoning them'. This was hardly surprising.

In Peter Cardew's account of crossing Sumatra, he recalled that, at Mariteboe, 'the Dutch were very helpful and fed us and somehow managed to procure a convoy of four buses'. At Sawah Lunto, 'the Dutch provided the whole 200 of us with a meal of hot stew at about one hour's notice and agreed to send us on by train the next morning. Their kindness was only equalled by their amazing efficiency'. At Padang, 'the Dutch again treated us with great kindness and Hughes and I were allotted a billet with a Eurasian family'.

Lieutenant W. J. B. Johnson of the RNVR did not have too much to say in favour of the party of Dutchmen in whose motorboats he and others were escaping from the island of Singkep. He acknowledged that they could not refuse to take the Dutchmen 'as the boats were really theirs', but found them 'complete passengers', though they made up for this by bringing quantities of food. However, the Dutch did work their passage eventually by having to bale water out vigorously all night from an overloaded boat. In Sumatra, Johnson was more than grateful for the kindness he received (see Chapter 5). There was a Dutch Controller who gave him food and rest and then took him to a hospital where the whole staff was up at 2 a.m. to look after him and operate on his leg. Finally, when he left the hospital, he recorded 'never having known such kindness' and hoped that one day he might be able to do something to repay the debt he felt he owed.

This may have been an extreme case, but there are several memoirs which tell of personal kindness and hospitality to the British and Allies who were escaping from Singapore. Martin Ogle, a former Education Officer from Penang, noted how well the Dutch authorities in Sumatra were handling a situation which they could not possibly have foreseen. Oswald Gilmour stayed with a Dutch family in Padang, prior to sailing for Colombo; he wrote later that he felt 'at a loss to describe the kindness and generosity of these people'. He also stated that the Dutch had not tried to evacuate their own nationals from the Netherlands East Indies as they had no other country to go to. They had made their homes in the Indies to a much greater extent than the British had done in Malaya, and there were far too many of them. 'It must', he concluded, 'have been galling to them to see hundreds of Britishers using the resources of the country to escape, while they could only wait to be captured'.

The British military officers on the Sumatran escape route realised their indebtedness to the Dutch authorities, even when allowance has been made for a measure of tact in anything they said publicly. Captain Gordon at Tembilahan stated that the Dutch were 'being splendid' and, at Rengat, Major Campbell was quoted as saying, 'the Dutch are doing wonders . . . they only have to forget us for a few days and we're finished'. At Padang, too, Colonel Warren worked closely with the Dutch authorities, attempting at a late stage to form a joint guerilla force with them. Earlier, he had to threaten drastic action against undisciplined British and Allied troops in the town and respond to allegations that some of them were attempting to sell arms to local people. Not everyone who was passing through in the hope of escape from western Sumatra behaved responsibly and there would seem, at times, to have been no shortage of grounds for complaint and resentment from the Dutch side.

From the British, there was an element of resentment, too, when some escapers or evacuees thought the Dutch should be doing more to help speed them on their way. Since the Dutch naturally controlled most of the resources, including road transport, petrol and the rail service to Padang, it was perhaps not difficult to ascribe delays to lack of effort on their part, whether the accusation was justified or not. A further area of potential friction was sometimes found in what were seen as attitudes of aloofness or indifference on the part of the resident Dutch. Mrs M. de Malmanche, who worked with the sick and wounded at Rengat, felt that she and other British nurses and doctors were ignored by the local Dutch population and, later at Padang, she was made sharply aware of a Dutch officer's angry accusation that the British had not fought at Singapore.

Whatever these sources of difference amounted to, on either side, they were not sufficiently damaging or widespread to have greatly disrupted the passage of British and Allied escapers and evacuees through Dutch colonial territory. The weight of the evidence appears to be very much the other way. Sometimes, undoubtedly, Dutch officials needed to think first of their own people, that is all those under their normal jurisdiction, in matters of transport and supplies. It might even be asked why, when they themselves would certainly face imprisonment under the Japanese, many Dutch and Dutch Eurasians continued to make major efforts to help others escape. There were other issues to be faced also. One was the pursuance of a 'scorched earth' policy to deny stocks and stores, and above all, the use of oil installations, to the incoming Japanese. Another factor in the situation was the uncertainty about the extent to which nationalist elements in the Indonesian population might appear ready to offer co-operation to the Japanese, if only to promote their own cause, and what this might portend for local Dutch families. As the pattern of

Japanese conquest proceeded in the Indies, the Dutch, both military and civilians, had more than enough problems to face without those created along the British and Allied escape routes from Singapore.

Some idea of how the Dutch in Java felt about their own situation during the early weeks of 1942 can be gained from an account written by Maria de Jonge, daughter of a former Governor-General of the Netherlands East Indies. As the Japanese forces advanced in South-East Asia, some Dutch women and children did leave Java for Australia and the USA, though, as the writer recalled, 'not nearly enough'. On the other hand, for their own greater security, many Dutch civilians 'poured into Java' from scattered locations in the outer islands. Great hope was placed on the Singapore 'fortress' to stem the Japanese advance; so many millions of pounds had been spent to make the island invulnerable. Then, within days, it fell, 'like a ripe plum into the enemy's mouth'. How could Java now be defended?

All available Dutch air force planes had, it was believed, been sent to the defence of Malaya and most had been shot down. It would only be a matter of time before the Japanese attacked Java, and a very short time at that; from the air, they would be able to strike wherever they chose. News of Japanese landings on the north coast of Java reached Maria de Jonge where she worked as a hospital matron in the Dutch capital, Bandoeing. She had lived close to government circles in both Batavia and Bandoeing and knew that there had been differing views on home defence policy in recent years. One school of thought held that a small army, operating in the Javanese terrain, might achieve most by adopting guerilla warfare tactics, rather than concentrating on a limited number of fixed defence positions. New military leadership, however, supported the opposite view and the Netherlands army was in the middle of a reorganisation process when it had to face its greatest challenge.

Battles for the major towns could only cause heavy civilian casualties, from bombing alone. Batavia was declared 'open' and capitulated on 3 March. Bombing and machine-gunning from aircraft became more frequent in Bandoeing, where troops, military supplies and large civilian population were all in close proximity. On 6 March, the Japanese demanded the surrender of Java, under threat of bombing Bandoeing 'out of existence'. As the Dutch government hesitated, the town centre was bombed, with resultant casualties. On 8 March, the Netherlands East Indies formally surrendered and several thousand troops took to the hills. It was only three weeks after the surrender of Singapore and the last rescue ship for evacuees and escapers had already left Padang in western Sumatra.

Although the scale of the situation was very much smaller, the Dutch authorities at Padang declared the town 'open' for much the same reasons as those which prevailed in Java. British and Allied forces arriving in the town along the escape route from the opposite coast of Sumatra were required to hand in their weapons, except that officers were allowed to keep their revolvers. Naturally, men who had carried their weapons this far did not all take kindly now to laying them down on the ground for collection. In situations of tension and frustration, British and Allied troops and civilians would sometimes relieve their feelings by complaining bitterly about the Dutch, a practice which applied equally the other way round.

As events moved to their inevitable outcome in the East Indies, many Dutch civilians in administrative or technical roles were facing an unprecedented dilemma as to how best to continue to serve their country and the local people. In very many situations, a local Dutch officer was on the spot, giving what help he could to refugees of all kinds and prepared to fill the lonely role of waiting for the Japanese to arrive. If such men appeared to be not always willing to see the last of the local boats disappear, this might have revealed obstinacy, or resentment or selfishness, but it might equally have meant a concern for those left behind, who had to go on living as best they could under new masters. It might be concluded, for instance, that when it came to late searches by small groups attempting to leave from the coast near Padang, the local Dutch administration could hardly have been expected to involve itself. This would have broken the 'open town' policy. Other things apart, in this particular situation neither Dutch nor Indonesians would have seen much prospect for success when small sailing craft in less than expert hands set out to challenge the might of the Indian Ocean.

A particularly difficult and delicate confrontation arose a few days after the start of a last-minute escape attempt in a junk from Padang.

The 'crew' had literally met on the quayside in the dark and managed to float the junk, the *Bintang Dua*, out into open water. Next morning, they discovered each other. There were four army officers, three navy men and 13 others, all soldiers, four of them senior NCOs. Captain Dudley Apthorp was the senior officer, but in his own later account, he recognised that they had lacked a leader with sea-going experience until they picked up another group of eight men in a small boat. Among these was Sergeant Strachino, engineer, soldier and seaman, who had at one time served on a coasting vessel out of Hull. Strachino's knowledge and experience were quickly recognised and, not without mishap and an element of mutiny and desertion, which are described later (Chapter 7), the *Bintang Dua* reached the southern entrance to the Strait of Siberut; ahead lay the Indian Ocean proper.

It was 30 March, two weeks after the *Bintang Dua* had left Padang. A small steamer approached through the strait from the north-west. The escape crew could only watch, and hope; the vessel carried no colours. At a distance of 200 yards, it circled round them and there was a burst of machine-gun fire, causing them to heave-to. A launch was lowered from the steamer and, as it came alongside, it could be seen that the men manning it wore hatbands of the Royal Netherlands Navy. They brought a message for the 'commander' to come on board the larger vessel, unarmed, and Apthorp and another officer named Purvis returned with them. The Dutch ship was the SS *Banggai*, 662 tons, and normally employed in servicing lighthouses round the Sumatran coast. The captain was Dutch and the crew Dutch/Indonesian and they were accompanied by, and subject to the orders of, a Dutch Commissaire of Police and seven armed Indonesian policemen.

Back in Padang, the owners of the *Bintang Dua* had complained to the Japanese, who were now in control there, that their boat had been stolen by a British escaping party and the *Banggai*, under police orders, had been sent out to recapture it and bring the British party back. Now, as the men from the *Bintang Dua* gradually transferred to the ship sent to recapture them, all the underlying attitudes, hopes and fears came to the surface.

Dudley Apthorp and his men had certainly not reached a stage where they were willing to give up their escape attempt; in a sense, the way ahead had just opened up for them. But the reality was that they were being held under armed guard. Taken back to Padang, they would face the distinct possibility of being executed by the

Japanese as escaped prisoners. The Dutch captain could not return to Padang, leaving the *Bintang Dua* and its crew to go free; this would have required the co-operation of the police, and there were too many witnesses to trust. Provided that he could obtain fuel and water, the captain indicated his personal willingness to go anywhere, even Colombo, but the Police Commissaire had a wife and children who were hostages in Padang. Other members of the crew and the police may well have been in similar situation and fearful of Japanese reprisals if they were, in effect, to join the escapers. In any case, what would have been the prospects for such a venture, seen from the point of view of the Indonesian members of the police or the ship's crew? There was a sense in which all those present were trapped by the circumstances in which they found themselves and the escape party prepared a plan to overpower the police, who were their guards, and take over the ship, hoping to carry the captain and crew along with them. Some felt that this move was almost being invited.

In the end, however, it was not put to the test. Dudley Apthorp was keen to try the plan, but unable to secure the full support he needed and without which, he realised, there was little chance of success. The *Bintang Dua* was towed to the island of Siberut, the *Banggai* turned eastwards and steamed towards Emmahaven, where they arrived next morning, 1 April. As they approached a white flag was hoisted on the ship and the escapers began to prepare themselves to face Japanese interrogation, a procedure on which their lives might well depend.

———————

In the defence of the Netherlands East Indies on the high seas, the Royal Netherlands Navy played a gallant, though tragic, role, which has been widely recognised. In the story of the fall of Singapore and the evacuations and escapes which followed, the Dutch merchant navy also made a very honourable contribution. The modern development of Dutch shipping in the Indies had been a fundamental factor in the promotion of trade, agriculture and industry, and in the inter-island migration of people, especially from densely populated Java to such development areas as southern and eastern Sumatra. Not only was this shipping important economically, it was equally vital to the process of political unification and efficient administration that officials, troops and mail could be carried securely throughout the Dutch territories. While civil air transport was developing before the Second World War, it was merchant shipping that still dominated the pattern of communication across the far-flung eastern empire of the Dutch in the 1930s. One large shipping company, the KPM (Koninklijke Paketvaart Mij), stood out among all the rest in the inter-island cargo and passenger traffic. Formed in 1888, the KPM had 45 ships in 1902 and 145 ships in 1930. In 1938, it accounted for about 70 per cent of the calls made in Netherlands East Indies ports by large steamers or motor ships. Before the war, the KPM was employing 1300 Europeans as ships' officers and another 800 in shore establishments. The crews of KPM ships included a force of 6400 Indonesians and 900 Chinese. A further 3000 Asians worked on shore for the company and its associated concerns. In Batavia, the company ran its own nautical school for officer training and promotion and, at nearby Tanjong Priok, it had a nautical institute which supplemented naval work in charting seas and rivers. With ships of various sizes and designs, catering especially for mixed cargo and passenger loads, the KPM carried all manner of goods and people, and even cattle and pigs. Even in the years of world depression it was a formidable and efficient organisation, which held on to as much business as it could; its merchant fleet was still in a strong position in 1941, both to continue normal trade and to respond to special needs arising from the wartime situation.

Before the surrender there, KPM ships passed in and out of Singapore, called at islands in the Rhio Lingga group, fréquented Bátavia and Tjiliatjap in Java, ánd Palembang, Oosthaven and Padang in Sumatra. One feature of KPM shipping policy had been a willingness to use very small landing points, jetties and roadstead anchorages. It was at such a place (Endraboera) on the west coast of Sumatra that a KPM ship put down naval Lieutenant W. J. B. Johnson so that medical attention could be urgently found for him. In some places, the company had even ran river-craft to connect with 'feeder' ships.

The KPM and other Dutch inter-island shipping formed part of a still larger range of water transport used in the Indies for trade and fishing purposes. This collection included Chinese junks and river boats, and local sampans and prahus. In the stories of escape and evacuation, all types of available craft played their part, for some a very tragic part. Dutch names appeared commonly among those of the bigger ships, which were making the longer runs and taking the larger numbers of passengers. Among them were the *Rochuissen*

(Singapore to Batavia), *Jagersfontein* (Batavia to Fremantle), *De Veert* (Padang to Colombo), *Duijmeyer van Twist* (Padang to Tjiliatjap), *Khoen Hoea* and *Zaandam* (Tjiliatjap to Fremantle), *Jalna Krishna* (Singapore to Batavia), *Palopo* (Padang to Colombo), and the ill-fated and tragic *Rooseboom* (Padang to Colombo, sunk by torpedo in the Indian Ocean). Dutch seamanship has a long and honourable history. In February and March 1942, these ships and their captains and crews added to it a further very honourable chapter by carrying so many evacuees and escapers from Malaya and Singapore on passages to freedom.

7 Small Vessels, Wide Seas

A number of British and Allied escaping groups from Sumatra attempted to cross vast stretches of ocean in sailing boats. Most of these brave expeditions headed westwards for India or Ceylon, though one boat sailed to the south-east in parallel with the coast of Sumatra, making, it was hoped, eventually for Australia. Only one of these sea-voyages was wholly successful, but another sailed well on the way to India before being intercepted by an armed Japanese naval tanker. A third adventurous sailing in the Indian Ocean ended by being blown so far to the east that the landing was made on the Tenasserim coast of Burma, already occupied at that time by the Japanese. Despite courageous efforts, other sailing boats did not reach far beyond the Sumatran coast.

Several small powered ships also made long ocean-voyages with military and civilian escapers and evacuees from Singapore; most were part of a second-stage movement from Sumatra or Java. These unlikely ocean-going vessels included Dutch KPM inter-island freighters, an erstwhile Japanese fishing boat and ancient Chinese river boats. These small craft were never meant for long, unbroken ocean routes, but many withstood the challenge and took their passengers safely, if slowly, to the sanctuary of a distant shore. The *Whang Pu*, a Chinese river steamer which made the voyage from Java to Australia has been mentioned earlier (see Chapter 3) and more attention is now given to SS *Palopo* and SS *Palimar*, from Padang to Colombo, the *Suey Sin Fan*, from the Indragiri river in Sumatra to Negapatam, southern India, and the *Wu Chang*, Java to Colombo.

One of the most remarkable escape attempts in a small sailing boat from Padang was undertaken by Flight-Lieutenant James Oswald Dykes and nine other servicemen, six British and three Australian. Dykes had been among the many late evacuees from Singapore who were bombed and shipwrecked at Pom Pong island. Picked up eventually by a small Chinese junk, he had reached first Singkep and then the Indragiri river in Sumatra. From Tembilahan, he travelled on a barge towed by a motor-launch, which reached Rengat on the evening of 25 February. Following an overnight stay in a Chinese school, Dykes was on his way again up-river to Ayer Molek, in what appears to have been, in the circumstances, a fairly smooth itinerary. There was a delay of a few days at Ayer Molek, a further stretch on the river and then a transfer to buses taking people to the Sawah Lunto railhead. Finally, he reached Padang on 6 March, to be quartered once more in a Chinese school. Colonel Warren, in charge of troops and troop movement in Padang, gave out that new arrivals could expect to wait for a few days until the navy called at the port and took them to Ceylon.

What neither Colonel Warren nor Flight-Lieutenant Dykes could know for certain at the time was that the chance of a naval rescue had already gone and the last of the Dutch merchant ships which might pick up evacuees and escapers was already on its way to Colombo. In fact, Colonel Warren did suspect that no more merchant ships would be calling. British naval ships had come into port five days earlier and taken off a large number of troops and civilians; it must have seemed unlikely that further naval help would be forthcoming, but there had to be hope. A week passed and the Japanese were regularly reported to be nearer. James Dykes was not the only bold spirit who was feeling restless. At mid-day on 16 March, those awaiting rescue in Padang were told that the town would be declared 'open' and would surrender to the Japanese, who could arrive that afternoon.

In the event, the Japanese did not arrive until the next day, but, by this time, Dykes had obtained permission for a small party to try to get away independently. It was a mixed group, like other small escape parties. There was one other RAF man, a leading aircraftman, the rest were soldiers, including three Australians and a British doctor, Captain H. M. Kilgour of the Royal Army Medical Corps. In the early afternoon of 16 March, this party made its way southwards along the coast to the village of Sungei Penang, where they had learned earlier that there was a boat available. Staying there overnight, they bought a boat for 550 Dutch guilders, around £80 at the time. James Dykes had a clear picture of the details. The boat was 27 feet long, with a maximum beam of six feet, and it drew two feet of water, with a freeboard of 18 inches. It carried a jib and mainsail and an outrigger, eight feet out on each side. The men took on board a supply of rice, bananas, water and firewood and set sail on the night of 17 March.

They made first for the island of Siberut, in the Mentawai group, to the west of Sumatra, and stayed there for a day or two to improve the condition of the boat and add to their supplies. The local Controller at Siberut and his son roofed over the hold of the boat in traditional style, strengthened the outriggers and the rigging and supplied several long bamboos as spare spars. The escape party was also given two sacks of rice, plenty of bananas and a good supply of water in four-gallon cans and bamboo containers. It was a splendid and heartening start, and this was not all. About a dozen food tins found by the Controller on the island were added to the stores and the boat crew left armed with useful information about the weather and sailing conditions. Dykes considered later that their safety had depended on the good workmanship put into the boat at Siberut.

As in all the small-boat escapes, there were good days and bad days, and usually much more of the latter. In the last week of March, this party encountered a variety of sailing conditions, strong head-winds against which they could make no progress, periods of flat calm, and times when they were going forward with favourable winds from force 2 to force 4. There were coral reefs to be negotiated near Batu Islands, where the boat sprang a small leak. At the beginning of April, they were in sight of the island of Nias and, helped by favourable winds, they sailed up its west coast to Seramoe, arriving there on 5 April, and beaching the boat while they sought further provisions.

Loaded with generous supplies of rice, tinned fish, bananas and 150 gallons of water, they had a struggle to get the boat off the beach and through the heavy breakers. A sudden squall on the 6th carried away the mast and sails, which were retrieved with difficulty; that night, the boat drifted. Next day, they beached again and rested on a small islet off the north-west corner of Nias. The mast had to be refitted and the sail mended. Meanwhile, one of the party, Lance-Sergeant Beaumont, Royal Artillery, was very ill with malaria and being looked after by the doctor. In this region, boiled hermit crabs and coconuts provided some variety in the diet.

On 18 April, they passed Simeleue, the most northerly of the main islands of the Mendawais. Winds had freshened to force 5 and 6, from the east, veering to the south, and the sea was rising. Sail was reduced but, with increasingly deep troughs in the sea and squally rain, conditions became very unpleasant. There was tragedy on 21 April, when an artillery bombardier, Bombardier Rawson, was lost overboard in the heavy seas, 35 feet high and winds up to force 7. In these conditions, there was no chance of a rescue. About the same time, the bowsprit was carried away. Sergeant Beaumont was still very ill and all the crew were weak and tired. The food ration worked out at one pound of rice, two small sardines and a pint of tea per head each day; they felt they dare not increase it. A tin of milk was retained for the sick man but time was running out for him and he died at 2.30 a.m. on 23 April. He was buried at sea half an hour later. From an original party of 11, they were down to nine and struggling again to repair the sailing equipment.

Islands were sighted to the north-east, thought to be the Northern Nicobars, and they found themselves sailing northwards up the west coast of a chain of islands, but unable to keep a track to the west of north. Instead, they found they were being blown to the east side of the islands; south-west winds were beginning to dictate their course. As the days ran on and April changed to May they continued to eke out their now meagre food supplies and remained weak and hungry. They caught sight of some distant shipping, possibly a small convoy in the distance, but did not know what nationality it might be. The winds continued from the west and south-west and the food and water supplies dwindled. Land was sighted at last on 13 May; wherever it turned out to be, it was essential they should make a landing very soon. They worked out that it was the coast of Burma and that they were heading north alongside it.

On the evening of 15 May, they made a landing and were able to buy some food the next day from local people. All had a good meal and felt better for it. There was a language problem as they were not able to communicate much with local Burmese, but it was evident that they were somewhere on the Tenasserim coast. Continuing their voyage northwards on the 17th the boat crew of nine men found themselves at one stage uncomfortably close to a small steamer flying the Japanese flag. By sunset, they had entered a river-mouth (it was the Salween) and had hidden the boat up a convenient creek.

Here, they found a Burmese who could speak Urdu and this allowed some communication. It transpired that they were seven or eight miles south of Moulmein and the Japanese were already in control of the whole area. James Dykes and his party had to accept, after two months of the most courageous struggle, that they had been defeated in their attempt to sail westwards across the Indian Ocean. They now gave their attention to the idea of reaching India overland; they would need more food and a guide and they asked the Burmese for help.

At mid-day next day, 19 May, food was brought, by prior arrangement, to a small hut in the neighbouring paddy fields. There was enough for only one meal and Dykes and his party argued with the Burmese that they also needed food to carry away with them. During these proceedings, an armed Japanese patrol approached and there was little alternative but to surrender. An Australian corporal did make a bolt for it and was not seen again. The eight survivors (of the original 11) were taken by motorboat to Japanese Military Police headquarters and then to Moulmein gaol. They had been at sea for two months, enduring great hardships and stress, and losing two lives, eventually probably a third one. They must have sailed a distance of some 1500 miles, virtually far enough to have reached Ceylon, with good fortune and good winds. Although they had failed in their objective, what they had achieved was astonishing enough and the reasons for failure are not difficult to judge.

It was late in the season for a sailing vessel of any kind to attempt a sea-crossing from Sumatra to southern India or Ceylon with the assistance of the north-east monsoon. Between March and April, the north-east winds would generally tend to become more variable, moving, by May, into a pattern which was more one of westerlies and south-westerlies. From May to October, the south-west monsoon is dominant in the region. When the *Sederhana Djohanis* set out on much the same voyage, it had many advantages over James Dyke's little boat. It was nearly twice as long and more than twice as broad in the beam. The vessel had a 'large head of sail' and a crew of 18 men, among whom there was considerable sailing experience. Yet, these men were concerned also that the monsoon might change and take them north-eastwards across the Indian Ocean, towards Burma. Dykes's party was held up by damage to their small boat and the time taken by necessary repairs. It was April before they were away from Sumatra and the islands off the west coast there, and not surprising, therefore, that, while they could make progress to the north, they had the utmost difficulty in trying to head for the west. They were weak, too, and often exhausted. 'We are rapidly being blown to the east', wrote James Dykes; they were also being blown back to fierce interrogation and imprisonment under the Japanese. The doctor's death, as a prisoner, followed shortly, from dysentery and malnutrition; he had been much respected by all in the boat party.

William Reynolds had been an Australian sea-captain who, in his own words, had 'swallowed the anchor' and settled to work in tin mining in Malaya. As war approached, he was first a member of the Local Defence Volunteers, then attached to the Royal Engineers as a demolition expert. In due course, he found himself heading south for

Singapore, blowing up tin-dredges, mining machinery, bridges and telephone exchanges on the way. By 10 February 1942, he considered it obvious that Singapore was going to be 'another Dunkirk' and, as no one appeared to want his services on the island, he took matters into his own hands. Choosing one of a number of diesel-powered Japanese fishing boats, he recruited a Chinese crew and prepared the vessel for sailing. During the period of the late evacuation of civilians and others from Singapore, and the subsequent bombings and ship-wrecks in the sea-passages to the south, Reynolds and his Japanese fishing smack were very active, taking people to the Indragiri river and then going back again into the islands to rescue more. There came a last trip to Rengat, where he was told he and his ship would be captured if he did not proceed to sea. Reynolds's Chinese crew had deserted a little earlier to a Chinese community among the islands; he recorded cryptically, 'we cast off, our objective this time being India'. To assist him on this ambitious voyage, he had two companions, Alex Elliott and George Papworth, who had been with him since Singapore. He named the vessel *Suey Sin Fan* (Lotus Bloom), after the abundant water-hyacinth on the Sumatran rivers, and made down the Indragiri into the Malacca Strait. Steaming by night and hiding in creeks masked by mangroves and fish-traps by day, they headed slowly westward, calling at the eastern Sumatran ports of Bengkalis and Bagan *en route*. They picked up a young Cantonese mother and her 3-year-old daughter and a 17-year-old Malay boy. By 26 March, they were off Diamond Point and shaping a course northward of the Nicobar Islands. From here, they 'hauled away westward for the long run across the Bay of Bengal'.

On the afternoon of 31 March they sighted the coast of India; soon they were at anchor in the roadsteads at Negapatam, six miles south of the port. They had crossed the ocean with a tiny crew of four or five, not counting the three-year-old. Reynolds was the only skilled seaman; Elliott had engineering knowledge. Madam Looi Pek Sye, the Chinese girl, had done the cooking 'when she was not too sea-sick' and taken the wheel whilst Reynolds got snatches of sleep. Reynolds rated her 'as good as two men in the crew' and called her journeying from Ipoh in Malaya to India, via Sumatra, 'an epic of courage and fortitude'. The Malay boy, from Kuala Lumpur, does not appear to have been mentioned again and it cannot be stated with certainty whether he had continued to India. The only navigational instrument which Reynolds had was a compass; for the rest, he relied on experience to make his judgements, and what he called 'a gigantic ego'. They had rested, he commented 'in the shadow of Allah'! It was a comment reminiscent of his earlier days, when he had captained ships taking pilgrims to Mecca. Reynolds arrived back in Australia and sent details of his rescue missions to Mrs Gretchen Howell, who was compiling lists of missing civilians. Tragically, about this time she heard of the death of her husband, Charles Howell, in internment in Taiwan; he had been Attorney-General in Singapore.

The experience of a military escape party from Padang under Captain (later Major) Dudley Apthorp was briefly recalled in the previous chapter. Their vessel, the *Bintang Dua* was located at Padang by chance and so was the crew, which came together, literally, in the dark. Like many others, Dudley Apthorp, who had been a liaison officer with 55 Brigade HQ, had arrived at Padang too late for a rescue ship. At Ayer Molek in Sumatra, he had stayed behind to help Colonel Dillon with the organisation of that stage of the Sumatran Escape Route, referred to sometimes as the 'Singapore Reinforcement Route'. One night, Captain Apthorp heard the Marines' Colonel Warren, say that there would be no more boats calling at Padang, which was to be surrendered to the Japanese with all Allied personnel. Warren himself felt he had no alternative than to stay for the surrender. There was still a large number of soldiers and civilians in the town and many were in hospital. Others could either stay with the Colonel, slip into the hills, or take to the sea. The latter option rested on being able to find a boat and a sufficient crew to handle it. It was the choice which Apthorp made and, down at the quayside, he and others on a similar quest first located a small motor-vessel, the *Banggai*. This had been sabotaged sufficiently that it was impossible to start the engine. A little further along, still in the darkness, a traditional Javanese junk was discovered, 50 feet long and the hold covered by an ark-like attap roof; it was the *Bintang Dua*. There were small decks fore and aft, the former having a cooking stove in the open, the latter providing meagre space for a helmsman and an assistant.

The self-appointed crew consisted of four officers and 16 others, four of these NCOs. There were three navy men, but no one had any real experience of sailing craft or navigation. It was 1300 miles to Colombo and the only chart on board showed a large island, Siberut, to the north of them. It was, it seemed, an obvious choice as their first target and should yield a supply of fresh water, if nothing else. One of the officers, named Purvis, was designated as captain because he knew a little about small boats. As they managed to move the junk out from the quay, rain came pouring down and nearly all took refuge below deck. In a rain squall, the mainsail split and, very shortly afterwards, a canoe-type boat came out in shallow water with eight ragged-looking men, who made their way on board. They were armed, but carried no food, 'just another hopeful escape group'. Their small boat was placed in tow behind the junk.

The new arrivals made a mixed contribution. Leading them was a Sergeant Strachino, who knew more about boats and seamanship than anyone else who had joined the *Bintang Dua* and was soon recognised as being in charge in that respect. The others proved to be a mutinous faction when the boat ran on to a reef. While the rest were struggling in the water to free the boat, five or six men made off with the canoe (or kayak), leaving the rest with no evident means of rowing to land. In the event, improvisation supplied a 'boat' and 'paddles', all made a landing and the *Bintang Dua* was recovered for repair. Astonishingly, the rebel party reappeared, but was driven off, Sergeant Strachino, threatening with a revolver. They were, however, allowed to keep the canoe with them and, with it a portion of the stores which had been loaded at Padang.

After two weeks, the *Bintang Dua* lay at the southern end of the Strait of Siberut and was preparing to leave behind the Mentawai Islands and head into the open waters of the Indian Ocean. It was at this point that the Dutch steamer arrived on the scene, as described in the previous chapter, with consequences already referred to. What might otherwise have happened to the *Bintang Dua* and its crew of 22 or so cannot be readily assessed, but they were still considerably to the south of the island of Nias and it was already late in the north-east monsoon season. What sailing speed might be maintained? How would food and water last out? Where might help be available? These were some of the imponderable questions, and could they reach a sufficient standard of seamanship to handle the navigational and other problems which they would meet? Even with a diesel-powered vessel and substantial earlier experience as a ship's captain, William Reynolds indicated a measure of relief when he reached the Indian coastline. The courage of those prepared to challenge the Indian Ocean in the *Bintang Dua*, like that of others who took out small boats to sail beyond the range of Japanese occupation, was quite remarkable, for the prospects were hazardous in the extreme. Dudley Apthorp and the men of the *Bintang Dua* survived the questioning and the threats of the Japanese at Fort de Kock, to be transported later to Medan, and thence to Burma and the building of the Burma – Siam railway, the notorious prisoner-of-war 'railway of death'. By the time they left Sumatra, Captain Apthorp was leading what was to be known as 'The Sumatran Battalion' of 480 men and 20 officers. In the miserably unhealthy and harsh conditions of those infamous railroad camps, and within the framework of Japanese control, this unit, and its commanding officer, was to create a legend of its own, which has been recorded elsewhere.

Another army captain who had left Singapore on the same boat as Dudley Apthorp, and who was in Padang at the same time, led a small escape group from the west coast of Sumatra. Captain 'Mike' Jennings of the Royal Engineers, mentioned earlier (Chapter 5), wrote his own account of a long sea-journey off the west coast of Sumatra. His plan was to sail in a southerly direction along the line of the Mentawai Islands, then follow to the island of Enggano, which he hoped he could use as a taking-off point for Western Australia. His was another last-minute departure from the coast near Padang. On the evening of 15 March 1942, he heard from another captain in the Engineers, James Thorlby, about the possibility of a boat. It turned out to be something of a dug-out canoe, 26 feet long and two feet in the beam. A party of ten men gathered with a view to venturing in this tiny craft, but they were not all equally enthusiastic, which was hardly surprising. One, a sergeant in an anti-tank unit thought the boat was unsuitable and went back to the town. A Eurasian member of the group left the boat as they got it into the sea. A third man also decided to leave just after the boat was launched. That left a group of seven, including the two army captains and a Bombardier Hall, who was to stick with Captain Jennings throughout. For the party was to split up during the passage through the friendly Mentawai Islands, and Jennings and Hall were to endure terrible suffering from the weather, hunger and thirst.

From Sipoera, their first island call, to arrival at Enggano covered a period of about two months and there were severe problems ahead, as the boat was to drift from day to day while the two men lay weak and often helpless. Eventually, nearly six months after leaving Padang, they landed on an island named Bayar, with the boat smashed in the breakers. Here they were picked up by the Japanese, taken to Benkulen and, eventually, to Palembang jail. By this time, it was late November, more than nine months since the surrender of Singapore.

Strange meetings and coincidences took place in the various theatres of escape. At Palembang, Jennings and Hall met one of the members of their original party which had started from Padang; none were free by this time. Stranger yet was the news that filtered through to Captain Jennings that his wife was held in internment in the Palembang area. She had served in the Medical Auxiliary Service in Malaya, reached Bangka at the time of the evacuation from Singapore and subsequently lived in the women's internment camps in Bangka and Palembang. Tragically, like many other women in those miserable camps, she did not survive the war, but died there in May 1945, three or four months before she and her husband could have been re-united.

J. S. H. Cunyngham-Brown, a Naval Reserve officer, was among those who attempted late escapes by sea from Padang and the neighbouring coastline. Earlier in life, he had 'run away to sea', and when war threatened in Malaya he had joined the Naval Reserve, while occupying the civilian post of Labour Controller in Johore. During and after the late evacuation period in Singapore, he was busy on rescue missions in the Malay Archipelago and the eastern coastal areas of Sumatra. Arriving, almost inevitably, too late for any rescue vessel from Padang, he was authorised by Colonel Warren to try to find a boat for a party of military staff officers, and then a second boat which he could utilise to lead an escape party of his own choosing. Colonel Warren provided money for the purchase of both vessels.

Cunyngham-Brown and a naval officer colleague, Robin Henman, were provided with two big cars to take the military party up the coast to the small port of Sasak, make all the necessary arrangements there and then return for a second group to sail in the second boat, also to be procured at Sasak. The first stage of this plan appeared to work well. There were several two-masted locally built schooners at Sasak. They were about 45 feet long, with open holds and thatched accommodation for the crew aft. After some hard bargaining with the local Malay fishermen, two of these boats were purchased and one was quickly provisioned with supplies of food and water. There was a fair range of sailing experience among the army officers who went on board and the two naval men saw them leave safely before starting to plan the departure of a second escape group.

Lieutenant-Colonel F. J. Dillon, who sailed as the senior officer in the sailing boat leaving Sasak, wrote his own account of these events and, while it agrees in substance with that of Cunyngham-Brown, there are differences in the details, which it seems safer just to summarise here. Because of the speed of Japanese troop movements, it became impossible to travel back to Padang again by road and the two naval officers were cut off and on their own. They still attempted to make use of the second large sailing boat which they had purchased, but during the night they were viciously attacked by a party of five local men who came out to them in a Malay prahu and offered to ferry them away safely from the Japanese, said to have just arrived in the village.

Cunyngham-Brown and Henman were lucky to escape with their lives and spent the next day or so trekking across sandbanks northwards to the vicinity of the next fishing village. Here they received real help from a headman who risked his own life by providing them with hospitality and supplying an outrigger dug-out canoe with single mast and sail, all of this taking place while Japanese patrols were scouring the area. The boat was only 20 feet long, but it was decided to sail it southwards along the coast, making back towards Padang and Emmahaven. If there had been no drastic change of circumstances, an escape party might still be waiting there for the two officers to return from Sasak. What would still be needed, however, would be a larger sailing vessel to replace what had been lost when they were attacked. But it was slow work. Not given to undue overstatement, Lieutenant Cunyngham-Brown put the duration of the voyage down the coast to Emmahaven harbour at six days and, when they arrived, the Japanese were only too obviously in evidence. The little sailing boat was turned to head north again.

Even the winds were now against them, at least close in-shore. Then, like many others, they met heavy rain-squalls and had problems with a torn sail and a leaky boat. Still hoping they might reach the Nicobars, but with nothing like adequate provisions, they were faced with frequent landfalls for repairs, food and water. In a desperate game of hide-and-seek among small islands and along the coastline, they were eventually captured and handed over to the Japanese authorities in Sibolga. They had reached a point somewhere to the north of the small port of Burus on the coast of western Sumatra.

Cunyngham-Brown was later to describe his imprisonment in Sibolga Jail and an expectancy of execution when the Japanese accused him of having joined with Indonesian guerillas against them. His protests that he belonged to the navy were, seemingly, swept aside and then, suddenly, he and Henman were literally thrown out of the jail, to be transported to the Medan area on the opposite coast, to a naval prison camp. He was a born survivor and, having first been involved in a serious road accident on the route over the hills and 'enjoyed' a short spell in hospital, he was later among the victims of a prisoner-of-war ship torpedoed in the Malacca Strait, *en route* from Medan to an uncertain destination. He fought for his life in the water, was picked up and landed in Singapore and eventually returned to Sumatra, to the miseries and dangers of a Pekan Baru 'death railway' camp. Meanwhile, his colleague, Henman, had been drafted to a road-making party in northern Sumatra.

More than one account has been published of the successful voyage of the Malay sailing boat *Sederhana Djohanis* which left the Padang area with a specially selected crew on 8 March 1942. Colonel Warren purchased the boat and eight of the crew of 18 had been at some stage in Special Operations work, while eight others were 'invited' in secrecy as individuals who might be particularly useful elsewhere in the war effort. A Chinese cook and a Malay orderly made up the total. It was a company of talent and skill, with a range of sailing experience. A local Asian crew accompanied them for a few days as they became accustomed to handling the boat and was then put ashore on an island visited by fishermen. The sailing plan was to work up the coast for about 200 miles and then make a westerly course for Ceylon. The boat was 45 feet long, carried two tall masts, had a beam of 16 feet and a draught of four feet; it had operated as a general local trading vessel. What was first required for success was a good run with the north-east monsoon across the Indian Ocean. For the rest, the requirements would include a disciplined crew, a careful rationing of food and water supplies and a strong element of good luck.

Richard Broome, a senior Malayan civil servant, was in charge,

Major L. E. C. Davies, RAMC, was ship's doctor and the naval officers on board included Geoffrey Brooke, who wrote his own account (in *Alarm Starboard*) later. John Davis, of the Straits Settlement police, was another member of this specially chosen company. They sailed some 1600 miles in five weeks, a remarkable achievement, for their vessel was no ocean greyhound and there were long days and periods of great anxiety, especially when they awaited a crucially favourable wind.

The story of the *Sederhana Djohanis* has been told elsewhere in detail. On 14 April, the small boat (and it was still a small boat in the vast ocean) was sighted by the *Anglo-Canadian*, a freighter of 5000 tons, which approached for a closer look. Looking down on the weather-beaten survivors from Singapore and Padang, the crew of the *Anglo-Canadian* could only be astonished at their discovery. For their part, the men of the *Sederhana Djohanis*, while very happy to be picked up on the freighter and taken on to India, felt a tinge of sadness as the Malay prahu which had brought them more than 1600 miles in five weeks faded from view. Two of the *Sederhana's* crew, Broome and Davis, were presently to return to Japanese-occupied Malaya on 'special operations' assignments.

There was nearly a second success for another traditional Malay boat, known as the *Setia Berganti*, which attempted to cross the Indian Ocean to Ceylon. This vessel sailed from Sasak, some distance north of Padang with a crew of ten, described by Cunyngham-Brown as the 'Fort Canning lot'. This was the mixed, but chosen, group from the services which Cunyngham-Brown and his colleague, Henman, had driven in large cars out to Sasak and then seen sail out. Lieutenant-Colonel Dillon was the senior officer and both he and Captain Ernest Gordon of the Argylls, who accompanied him, had assisted in the running of the evacuation route through Sumatra. Others included Edward Hooper, Naval Reservist and chosen to be skipper, another naval officer, a merchant navy officer and army officers from Signals, Artillery and Engineers. An Air Force Reservist who was normally a planter, and a Singapore businessman who spoke Malay and Dutch made up the ship's company. Not all who were invited had accepted, which is not surprising when Dillon's own early estimate of the chance of success was only ten per cent, a figure which he lowered before departure. On the other hand, one of those who accepted said he would rather be dead than a prisoner (he died as a prisoner in Thailand later) and another, on being asked to join this party, exclaimed, 'My God! I thought you were going to leave me out!' An army doctor declined the voyage in order to stay behind with sick and wounded.

It had been thought that a number of reasonably sized sailing luggers, with auxiliary engines, lay berthed at Sasak. These were normally used by the oil companies, plying up and down the coast, and to and from adjacent islands. In fact, the oil companies had recently destroyed all boats of the auxiliary-engine type, leaving only the Malay sailing craft, minor vessels of local design. It was just as well that there was plenty of sailing experience among the selected crew for the *Setia Berganti*, but the only navigational aids they carried were a compass, a school atlas and a naval book of nautical tables.

Colonel Dillon was very much a supplies and organisation officer and, in a very short time, the boat on which their lives would depend was well provisioned with food and water. The water was boiled on the beach first and amounted to 700 gallons, held in cleaned-out petrol and oil cans and drums. With rationing, it was expected to last a month and would be replenished whenever possible through island calls. Ballasting was carried out with sand and baulks of timber. The local population may have been impressed by all this activity, but not to the point of having much faith in the success of the voyage. As rice, coconuts and fresh fruit, in various stages of unripeness, were taken aboard, and a small dug-out light canoe, which could just take three men, was strapped to the deck, some of the local fishermen made it quite clear that they thought the whole enterprise was crazy. On 17 March, local help in poling got the *Setia Berganti* over the harbour bar and this was followed by cries of 'good-bye' from the beach, the intonation carrying a very realistic ring.

A first call was made at the island of Pini and, subsequently, a local pilot helped the crew to reach the island of Tana Masa, 40 miles to the north-east, where a sleeping deck was made and added to the prahu. The sailing vessel was hardly longer than 30 feet overall and had a steeply rising stern, where the steersman sat and manipulated a big rudder by means of a tiller bar. There were two masts, a bowsprit, with jib and foresail, and an enormous mainsail, with a boom reaching from the foremast for about 10 feet right over the stern of the ship. There were obviously problems for the uninitiated in handling a bulky vessel of this description, but other problems arose too. Those who had gone ashore at Pini had picked up symptoms of malaria and went down with the disease one after the other. At Tana Masa, the crew was called upon to arbitrate in a local feud among the islanders and, as they made slow progress out beyond Nias and towards the northern point of Sumatra, Dillon was conscious of the spread of some feelings of reluctance to continue.

However, continue they did into the open ocean and spirits seem to have risen again. They appeared to have avoided any danger of enemy attack while off, or near to, the Sumatran coast and to have sailed beyond the reach of Japanese aircraft. A possible submarine presence and the associated threat of torpedoes still remained, but each day took them further westwards across the wide sea. According to Ernest Gordon, when they calculated distances roughly, they were less than 500 miles from Colombo. Colonel Dillon took out a bottle of old Tokey wine, which he had kept for the purpose, and they had a preliminary celebration.

It was too soon! Next day, they saw the funnels of three ships, tankers, heading north-east. They could only be Japanese. In mist and rain at the time, the tankers passed the *Setia Berganti*, no more than half a mile away. Had they been seen? The answer seemed at first to be 'No', but out of the mist the tankers turned and came again, first one and then the others. A shot came over the sailing boat and they hove-to.

They were naval tankers, of about 10 000 tons, in battleship grey, which had been engaged in refuelling a Japanese fleet in the Indian Ocean. One of them, the *Sinkoku Maru*, towered over the now very small *Setia Berganti*. A rope ladder was put down, the erstwhile escaping party was taken aboard at revolver-point, held prisoners and interrogated. Four days later, they were back in Singapore, left at the quayside to be picked up by an army lorry and taken to Changi. The *Setia Berganti* had drifted away, meanwhile, in the Indian Ocean.

It had been a rare chance that the Japanese tankers had come so close and that there had been just enough light for the Malay prahu to be spotted. It was the difference between freedom and imprisonment for those on board.

An ancient Chinese river-steamer, SS *Wu Chang*, left Tjiliatjap in southern Java on 27 February 1942. On board were more than 500 services and civilian personnel, remnants of military, naval and air force units from Singapore and Java, and a random collection of other people. They found themselves sailing westwards, bound for Colombo. Many of these passengers had earlier been evacuated from Singapore to Sumatra, made the journey there from east coast to west coast and been collected by HMS *Danae* at Padang and brought to Tjiliatjap. Among them was Colonel B. H. Ashmore, who recorded the temporary use by servicemen of a transit camp at Powokerto, about 25 miles inland from Tjiliatjap; after three days there, they were all back on a train again, returning to the port. It was yet another evacuation, following the break-up of the Allied HQ in Java on 26 February, and they were now sailing again. Colonel Ashmore had originally left Singapore on the minesweeper SS *Malacca*, with a permit and orders to report to the regional military HQ in Java, but, following bombing attacks on the approach to the Bangka Strait, they had diverted to the estuary of the Indragiri river, picking up survivors from other attacks and shipwrecks during the night as best they could. Ashmore had now reached Java after all, but via the west coast of Sumatra and on a naval cruiser!

The *Wu Chang* was not only an old boat, but it had not been built for voyaging on the high seas. The vessel was flat-bottomed and it rolled horribly. There had been rumours of moving in convoy, but the ship's captain, Commander Cromarty RNVR, decided to go it alone, steering his own course. The voyage to Colombo was expected to take up to 10 or 11 days and food and water had to be carefully rationed. There were no lifebelts on the ship, only three lifeboats and a few bamboo rafts. A continuous look-out was kept for aircraft and submarines, but the first three or four days remained uneventful. Conditions were overcrowded and uncomfortable and the days were tedious, but no worse than that.

On 4 March, at 11 a. m., a Japanese submarine was sighted. Two, possibly three, torpedoes were fired at *Wu Chang*. The flat bottom of the old river-boat almost certainly saved the crowded vessel; two torpedoes passed underneath. A submarine then surfaced, not more than 100 yards away, travelled east about 300 yards and dived. Next, it was seen on the horizon, emitting smoke, probably discharging the batteries. Everyone on board the *Wu Chang*, recalled Colonel Ashmore, expected a second attack and thought it was the end. They were hundreds of miles from land and had only three boats. The old steamer continued to plough the sea full-out and, in a long, tense period, nothing further happened. Neither crew nor passengers knew that three days earlier, on the same passage, the 1000-ton *Rooseboom* had been torpedoed and sunk, with almost total loss of life. After two hours waiting, they returned to the normal daily routine. It was imagined that the submarine must have fired her last torpedoes, had no gun and needed to charge her batteries. It had been a very lucky escape.

Great praise was due to the captain and his crew for the handling of the *Wu Chang* in such difficult and dangerous circumstances. The old boat and its passenger load arrived safely in Colombo harbour on 9 March, the same day on which a Dutch steamer, the *DeVeert* arrived from Padang. From those disembarking, there was not only a sense of profound gratitude to the captain; there was also a real feeling of affection for his ship.

A little earlier, steaming in exactly the opposite direction, south-west to Australia, was another old flat-bottomed Chinese river-boat, *Whang Pu*, carrying passengers and 71 crates of Malayan Survey Department map materials, salvaged from Kuala Lumpur and Singapore. Originally part of a convoy of ten ships, the *Whang Pu* left Batavia on 19 February and sailed through the Sunda Strait at night. It was a new adventure for this old boat to be chugging through a great ocean and there was little comfort for the passengers, except for the thought that each day brought them nearer to the comparative safety of the Australian coastline. They also experienced a torpedo attack which missed them; these vessels, it seems, despite their lack of speed, did not offer the easiest of targets. With relief for all on board, the *Whang Pu* entered Fremantle Harbour on 2 March. By this time, another small steamer, SS *Palimar* had left Padang for Colombo in the early hours of a day (1 March) which was to witness the British naval rescue operation there by destroyers and cruisers. Captain J. R. C. Denny, of the Queen's Own Royal West Kent Regiment, kept brief notes of this voyage and his own experiences which led up to it. Together with three other British officers and 11 British and Indian other ranks, he had sailed from the island of Tekong, off the north coast of Singapore, on the night of 15 February. They were handling a powered Chinese junk which had been on duty with the Royal Engineers. Reaching Tanjong Pinang (Rhio) next afternoon, they were offered a tow by a Dutch motor vessel; already there were seven Australian and three British soldiers on the Dutch boat.

Not without some setbacks, which included the sinking of the junk, Captain Denny, recognised as leader because of his knowledge of boats and local languages, got this party to Sumatra and found himself in the Abadir School in Padang on 23 February. He would appear to have been a day ahead of Colonel Warren, who came to take charge of military movements, but he met Brigadier Paris, who was to go to his death on the *Rooseboom*. How Denny himself escaped this fate is not clear, but he was in Padang for about a week while rumours of shipping went round and he took part in a number of 'stand-to's' and 'stand-downs'. In a sea-crossing which took 9 or 10 days, *Palimar* got him away safely to Colombo in the end. Water was scarce and the food was a steady diet of rice, bully-beef and sardines. Submarine spotting was one of the regular deck duties, but the only naval vessel observed was a British destroyer, on 9 March. Next day, they were safely in Colombo harbour.

———————

The last rescue ship out of Padang (other than the sailing boats) was the SS *Palopo* (mentioned in Chapter 4), a small freighter which had left Java rather late and called in at Emmahaven for fuel. The date was 5 or 6 March, and just at that time Padang does not appear to have been overcrowded with refugees. Both the navy and the *Rooseboom* had taken off large numbers, services and civilians, within the previous seven days, and, between the two, SS *Palimar* took off others in the early hours of 1 March. Transport problems and a flooded river were temporarily slowing up movement along the Sumatran evacuation route. This was the time when the staging point in the rubber estate at Ayer Molek reached a peak figure of about 1000 people in transit. The *Palopo* picked up 50 people, 38 servicemen and 12 civilians. Colonel Warren made known that it was a small ship, but it might also be the last to come in and it appears he was right. He advised those who could do so to take it.

The *Palopo* could only manage a top speed of nine or ten knots and was very vulnerable on leaving port. Fortunately, it was a cloudy day and the usual Japanese reconnaissance plane did not appear. They sailed through Siberut Strait at night and, after three days at sea, sighted and picked up two Asians on a raft. They were survivors of another evacuee ship from Padang, a grim reminder to those on *Palopo* of what might still befall them. But they steamed slowly on and on and eventually reached Colombo. It was perhaps appropriate that, though the number of passengers was fairly small, the categories among them were varied. These included British and Australian soldiers, two Indian army officers, members of the Straits Volunteers and civilians from government service in Malaya. It was also fitting that the senior military officer on board was a Colonel Cummins, one of the two VC's of the Malayan Campaign.

Mr Gilmour, (mentioned earlier) who had been a municipal engineer in Singapore, published his own memoirs of this period as early as 1943. At the end of his book, he asked, 'how does a man assess his fortune? Not long before, I had a good job, considerable savings, a pleasant house . . . and all the usual valued things one gathers in half a lifetime. So far as I knew, all were lost . . . and of all that I had in Singapore there remained to me now only ragged shorts and shirt, broken canvas shoes, my identity disc, my passport, my wallet, containing a Dutch guilder, an identity card, my pass to leave Singapore and a blurred snapshot of my wife and child. Yet, that night [when he reached Colombo], I thanked God as I had never done before for all that was left: for life, freedom, family, friends, the health and the will to start again.'

G. J. O'Grady was also among the lucky 50 who escaped on the *Palopo*, but it could certainly be argued that he deserved his good fortune. A long-serving Public Works engineer in Malaya, he had made great efforts to return from leave in Australia when the Japanese invaded the country. He had arrived in Singapore in mid-January 1942, been evacuated on the *Kuala* a month later and been bombed and shipwrecked at Pom Pong island. He and other engineers had helped refugees on Pom Pong and other islands and, in due course, he had reached the line of the Indragiri River in Sumatra. At Rawang, where he made his first stop along the river, he heard an account of how British officers had been 'sent over' as early as 3 February to establish a string of posts along the route which he was now following. For part of his journey up-river, he was on board a hospital motor-boat, but he arrived at the rubber plantation at Ayer Molek on one of four barges which had been towed along the river.

Falling in with a planter from Johore, a man named Grant whom he knew, he secured the permission of the local Dutch Controller to purchase 15 gallons of petrol and, armed with this, made an agreement with a Malay who had an old, battered hire-car to drive them onwards over the mountain pass to Sawah Lunto, starting at dawn next day. It was an adventurous car ride. The car engine stopped from time to time and the radiator boiled. Worst of all was a stretch of road, about a hundred yards long, where flood water lay four feet deep. They waited for the water to go down, which it did slowly, and then gently eased the car through as soon as possible, but while it was still deep. Their luck held and they reached a Rest House at Sawah Lunto at 1.30 a.m. Three hours later, they were on a train for Padang, where they were billeted in the Christian Brothers' Mission House.

They were now in contact with Colonel Warren and, during the next night, were instructed, with others, to walk down to the railway station in well-spaced groups of two or three, and not to ask anyone the way, or seek any taxis. It was pitch-dark, with a black-out in force, and after a long, quiet walk through the town, they boarded a blacked-out train, which took them to a jetty. Here, they arrived, in great secrecy, at 3 a.m. and found a Tamil boy selling oranges and soft drinks to departing passengers!

Mr O'Grady described the *Palopo*, moored at the jetty, as 'un-attractive', but 'a grand, faithful old tub', which he would remember for the rest of his life. Mr Gilmour had remembered that the little ship was covered everywhere with coal-dust when he went on board. The last steamship to leave Padang before the Japanese forces arrived crept out to the wide open and dangerous waters of the Indian Ocean at a placid six knots. Passengers slept on the hard deck or the hatches, sometimes burned by the sun, sometimes swept by wind or rain. Twice a day, there was a dish of rice and herrings, together with a mug of hot tea; a ration of five cigarettes a day was also issued.

One afternoon, they passed through 'the flotsam of a lost ship, bits of wreckage, empty lifebelts covered with green slime and the body of a woman, face down, with one leg missing'. What seemed at first to be a bundle of rubbish turned out to be two survivors, a Malay and an Indian. (These were 'two Malays' in Gilmour's account, more cor-rectly, perhaps, Javanese crew members.) They waved feebly. For nine days, they had squatted on a tiny gimcrack raft, without food, living only on rainwater, caught in cupped hands. As O'Grady put it, 'a clumsy European would have toppled off such a frail support a hundred times'. He came to realise that the stricken vessel had been the *Rooseboom* which had carried his head of department, Major R. L. Nunn, and his wife, both good friends of O'Grady.

In all the incidents relating to escapes and evacuations, there was no way of determining where the best chances lay. Those who had left on the *Rooseboom* must have felt they had made good time since their departure from Singapore, despite shipwreck on the way in some cases; yet all but four of more than 500 perished in the Indian Ocean. O'Grady and Grant had been so exhausted that they had stayed overnight back at Rawang, their first stage on the Indragiri, when it would have been possible for them to continue up-river. They had also, with many others, endured a slow passage on heavily-laden river barges. But they had risked the use of a hired car and faced a dangerous stretch of floodwater on the road. Consequently, they arrived at Padang too late for the ill-fated *Rooseboom*, but in time for the unprepossessing, but wholly worthy *Palopo*, which arrived safely in Colombo.

O'Grady needed a spell in hospital, then he was on board a ship to Mauritius and, finally, from there to Fremantle and Perth. Four months had passed since he left his leave-base in Australia and three months since he left Singapore. It was May 1942, when he cabled his wife, traced in Melbourne, to send £30 to him, back at Perth. She cabled back with her love and £50; it was a fitting reply.

8 Mainland Escapes

As the Japanese army and military police came to extend their control over the Malay Peninsula the chances of a late escape by any Europeans still at large there were very small. While in British hands, Singapore had been the focus for a major retreat on the part of both troops and civilians. For the short period of two weeks between the end of the fighting on the Peninsula and the fall of Singapore, the island still offered some hope for those left behind who were bold and resourceful enough to make an escape bid. After 15 February 1942, Singapore, too, was Japanese-occupied territory and no longer part of any obvious escape-route.

In what might be seen as a short 'twilight' period between the successes of the Japanese army and the firm establishment of a military administration in Malaya and Singapore, a certain amount of escape movement took place between places on the west coast of Malaya and the east coast of Sumatra. The strategy was still that of attempting to reach an ocean-going port in Sumatra, or even in Java, and take ship from there. No one could predict exactly how long it might take the Japanese to conquer these areas, or even whether a stage might soon be reached where the Japanese advance would be checked. In the event, the Japanese maintained a pace of advance well beyond what most could possibly have foreseen. As the prospects of any successful voyage from Malaya to the Indonesian islands disappeared quickly (though a vision of such an escape route remained for much longer), there was only one immediate course open to Europeans (a term used here to include Australians and New Zealanders) and this was to take to the cover of the jungle. It was clear that Europeans could not live freely and openly under a Japanese wartime regime; even Eurasians were becoming increasingly 'suspect' and were persecuted and interned. It was also soon made clear that severe penalties, usually death, would be inflicted on Asian peoples who attempted to protect or assist European refugees, military or civilian.

There were some outstandingly heroic cases where Malayans of different races helped Britons and others, at the risk of their own lives, but these situations could not last for long and the continued freedom of Europeans came to depend very much upon their association with jungle encampments of guerillas, very largely Chinese in both membership and leadership. British and Allied soldiers who took to the jungle, together with planters, tin miners, district officers and others soon found their freedom of action circumscribed by the routines of guerilla camps and the harsh regulations and discipline maintained in most of them. There were limits to what might be attempted by individuals or small groups of would-be escapers and even that most legendary of British stay-behind officers. Colonel Spencer Chapman, noted in a later report that 'once I had joined AJUF [a combination of anti-Japanese guerilla fighters and helpers living outside the jungle], my freedom of movement was limited'. It would seem that only in the later stages of the Japanese Occupation, when frequent air-drops brought weapons and other supplies to the guerillas, and preparations were in hand for an invasion of Malaya, did British leadership seriously challenge the dominant role of the Chinese in the guerilla camps.

From north to south, on each side of the main mountain range in Malaya, there was a mass of dense jungle, coming down, in places, to meet stretches of mining land and plantation agriculture. The main trunk routes lay on the western side of the mountain range and ran from north to south; there were few good east–west crossings. Overland to the north, Thailand and Burma came under Japanese control together with the former French colonial territories which once bore the title of 'Indo-China'. For Europeans, there was not much chance of a practical escape route to the north, though some did think in terms of reaching Burma and India. Distances were great and conditions too difficult to encourage much real hope in that direction, but not all who hoped to escape were realists. Among the thousands of British and Allied prisoners who travelled from Singapore to Thailand to work on the notorious 'death railway', there were certainly some who dreamt of a way out to the north-west. For the record, one Chinese man did succeed in making his way from Singapore through Malaya and Thailand, to reach south-west China, where he was closely questioned about the morale of the Chinese in Japanese-occupied Malaya. But this was a very exceptional experience and scarcely within the bounds of possibility for a European. Guerilla camps and groupings in Malaya moved frequently, according to circumstances, but, in general, jungle areas of Perak, Selangor, Johore and Pahang provided the main locations, with further bases in the north-east states, where Japanese control tended to be looser.

In a classic account of anti-Japanese activities from bases in the Malayan jungle, Colonel F. Spencer Chapman described the jungle

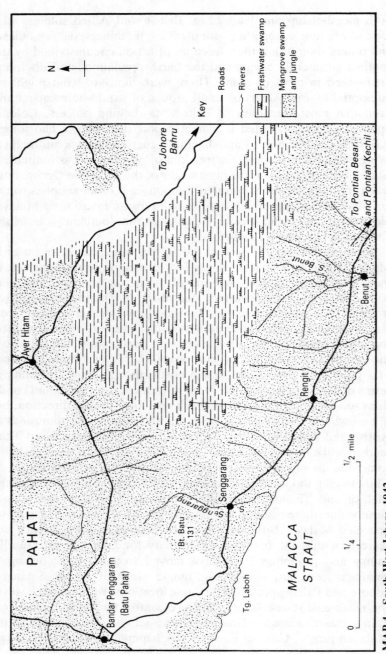

MAP 4 South-West Johore, 1942

as 'neutral, neither friend nor foe in itself', but it was dark, damp and unhealthy, and could quickly test Europeans to the limits of survival. Many took to the jungle for freedom's sake and ended by dying there. For stay-behind troops, the jungle offered the prospect of cover from which attacks on Japanese lines of communication could be planned. Many envisaged a temporary refuge only, until the counter-offensive was on the way from Singapore. That hope died when news of the fall of Singapore filtered through. Staying in the jungle then became essentially an alternative to the prospect of capture and imprisonment by the Japanese, or, perhaps, death at their hands. A more lingering death from malnutrition or other diseases remained a very distinct prospect.

Shortly before the Japanese invasion of Malaya, a 'special operations' unit was set up in Singapore to train men for fighting and undertaking sabotage operations behind enemy lines. Short, intensive courses at this 101 Special Training School brought together British and Allied officers and Asian volunteers, the latter mostly Chinese. Altogether 165 Chinese members of the Malayan Communist Party received 'special operations' training in Singapore between 21 December 1941 and 22 January 1942, and a further 25 members of the Chinese Nationalist (Kuomintang) Party had been selected for training when the school was scheduled to close down. The scale of this preparation for wartime activity in a Japanese-occupied Malaya was modest and the timing of everything was late, but it was particularly significant for the promotion of initiative and leadership and for the measure of co-operation achieved between a small team of British officers and the leaders of a largely Chinese guerilla movement.

On the British side, mine managers, planters, district officers and others whose territories were over-run during the Japanese advance down the Peninsula sometimes became part of the stay-behind organisation through force of circumstances. Working and living in small groups, usually in contact with regular officers, and supported by Chinese volunteers, they found a role and a sense of companionship to counter the great dangers to which they became exposed. Trapped, in some cases, by time and place, any choice of action for such men was stark enough and rumours of Japanese treatment of captured Europeans may already have been circulating.

Hugh Travers Cummins was managing a tin mine in southern Thailand when the first Japanese landings took place there. He was arrested by the Thai police and handed over to the Japanese military authorities. He soon found himself in a group of 27 Europeans, 22 of them British. They were quickly transferred to another tin mine site and held prisoner in a bungalow; 12 Indian prisoners-of-war, presumably taken on, or near, the Thai border were brought in to add to the numbers. From the total company, three Danes, a Swede and a Pole were judged to be 'neutrals' and allowed to leave. Three Indian NCOs were taken out and shot. The Japanese guards then attacked the rest of their prisoners, using grenades, a machine-gun and automatic rifles. This attack was from outside the building, but was followed by the entry of the soldiers, to use their bayonets on anyone still showing signs of life. Somehow, six of the prisoners survived this ordeal sufficiently to leave the bungalow that night and make for the jungle fringe. *En route*, they met up with the five 'neutrals' who had been allowed to go free. But this was now rather a large party and they split up. Mr Cummins, one of the survivors, trekked largely on his own for six weeks. He had shrapnel in his head and legs and a bayonet wound in his foot; he had been left for dead. The hospitality of small village communities who gave him food and temporary shelter helped him to keep going, but by the time he had reached southern Kedah, he was utterly exhausted and gave himself up to the local Malay administration. Transferred to the Japanese military authority, with an accompanying plea for his life, Cummins spent the next year in gaol in Alor Star and was finally transported to Singapore.

Perhaps eight out of the 11 people who made their way from the earlier scene of the massacre at the bungalow were still able to survive. Two reached as far south as Ipoh, a remarkable achievement, before giving themselves up, exhausted and suffering from beri-beri. These two spent time in gaols in Ipoh and Kuala Lumpur and only one eventually reached the Changi internment camp in Singapore. They were desperate people who never had any real chance of escaping, but they could initially have had no means of assessing how for and how quickly the Japanese advance had continued. They must have harboured hopes of a counter-offensive from the south, which might yet liberate them. Weakened by long journeys on foot in the tropical humidity, and living on an inadequate diet, they were vulnerable to tropical diseases, especially in swampy areas, where leech bites added another great source of misery and infection. Only will-power could have sustained those who made their way as far south as Ipoh.

The east coast state of Trengganu had a long coastline, but no railway and few roads. Jungle, mountains and rivers characterised most of a region where, away from the coast, the patterns of human settlement were small and scattered. Within two or three days of the initial Japanese landings further north, some British expatriates working in Trengganu reached the conclusion that they were being cut off. The road which led northwards from Kuala Trengganu to Kota Bharu formed a junction with an east–west route at Pasir Puteh, just over the border in Kelantan; it was known on 10 December 1941 that defending troops had withdrawn from this junction, leaving the way open to Japanese forces pressing south from Kota Bharu.

At the same time, news was received in Kuala Trengganu that Japanese landings had taken place further south, at Kuantan, where, it was reported, the invaders were 'being held'. It seemed that if the British group took either main route from Kuala Trengganu, they would meet advancing Japanese forces, while to stay where they were would mean certain imprisonment at least. It was decided instead that they should try to reach Kuala Lipis in Pahang by a journey through the jungle, using rivers and mountain paths and crossing a mountain range. It was a journey said to have been attempted only three times previously by Europeans, and each time in dry weather. Now, the monsoon had broken before the party could set out.

A total of 17 Britons accompanied by three Malay guides made the whole journey and some temporary Malay help was engaged to help build overnight shelters or rafts for a river. The British party included five men from the Malayan Civil Service and officials from Education, Customs and Public Works. There was a Chief of Police and his wife, and another woman whose husband was away, serving in the Volunteers. A third woman in the party was Dr Cecily Williams who was holding the unusual State appointment of lady doctor. A flight-lieutenant from RAF ground staff was the lone serviceman in the group, but George Patterson of the MCS had been commissioned in the Royal Artillery in England and was a captain in the Local Defence Volunteers. His platoon had just been engaged in rounding up Japanese residents in the Dungun area and transporting them to Kuala Trengganu.

It was decided initially that some members of the party would drive south along the coast road to Dungun, pick up boats there and proceed up-river to Jerangau; there they would rendezvous with the others who made for Jerangau by road. Nothing made for quick movement, as the coastal route involved rather old-style ferry cross-

ings over rivers and, further inland, it took cars five hours to cover
the 40 miles or so from Kuala Trengganu to Jerangau. Here, three
small groups were determined and food supplies split between them.
Captain Patterson led the first group and it is his report which is
followed here. His was to be the advance group, setting the pace; the
second group was to move at the speed of the two women in it and
the third group was to follow in easy stages. It was hoped that the first
arrivals at Kuala Lipis would be able to send motor boats up the
Tembeling river to meet others and bring them through the later
stages of the journey. Meanwhile, the means of transport would vary
from the poling of shallow-draught boats and the sailing of bamboo
rafts, according to the flow of the rivers, both activities involving
Malay assistance, and trekking on foot along jungle paths.

There was heavy rain on the way, rivers became swollen and
bridges, consisting of a single tree, became hazardous to cross; one
member of the leading group fell twice into water ten feet below.
Where the jungle came right down to a river in flood, they walked in
the river itself. They had left Jerangau on 12 December and, by the
night of 14 December, they were camping at 3000 feet. Afterwards, it
was downhill, but the going was no easier as they joined the Tembeling where it was high and fast-flowing; bamboo rafts were used in a
mixture of speed and adventure. As they entered the broader waters
of the river, they met two large motor-boats bringing a search party
sent out by the Resident of Pahang. Ironically, one member of this
party was the Forest Officer from Trengganu who had been stationed
in the south near the Pahang border and who had found out that the
report of Japanese landings at Kuantan was completely false!

After about five days of jungle travel, the whole party which had
come through from Jerangau had joined up again and all were well, if
weary. They had successfully completed a route which was more
reminiscent of the experience of some nineteenth-century pioneers.
'The women,' recalled Mr Patterson, 'were marvellous' and, of one
of them, he added that she was 'tall, elegant and cheerful, setting out
in clothes and footwear clearly not designed for jungle trekking'.
Where the Tembeling came close to the Pahang railway, the party
left the river to join a freight train and reached Kuala Lipis railway
station on the evening of 18 December. To his great annoyance,
George Patterson found they were faced with a demand for 3rd class
rail fare for the freight-car part of their journey. The jungle crossing
had demanded courage and stamina, but it solved little in the end.

Within the space of the next two months very few of those involved escaped imprisonment under the Japanese.

Robert Chrystal and William Robinson were both planters from estates in Perak, who joined the stay-behind organisation in Kuala Lumpur after their estates, further to the north, had been over-run. They were given commissioned rank in the army for 'behind the lines' operations and had to face the difficulties and dangers involved in attacking Japanese road convoys, living and hiding in the jungle and working out a relationship with Chinese guerillas in Selangor and elsewhere. Chrystal, a Scot from Glasgow with 24 years' experience as a planter, survived the war period of $3\frac{1}{2}$ years in the jungle. At one time, he lived on his own for nine months and came very close to death. Robinson was destined to die in the jungle, as were two other British men, Vincent Baker and Brian Tyson, from the Sungei Lembing tin mine in Pahang. Commonly, men went down with fever, malaria, beri-beri and general malnutrition.

Japanese armed patrols were frequently active against the Europeans hiding in the jungle and the Chinese guerillas with whom they co-operated. Clark Haywood, an electrical engineer from Kuala Lumpur, was killed in an encounter with Japanese troops, and three planters, Bill Harvey, Frank Vanrennan and Richard Graham, all active in Perak in the early stages of the Japanese Occupation, were taken prisoner and housed in Kudu Gaol, Kuala Lumpur. Here they found themselves in shared cells in very confined quarters in the general company of a large number of British and Allied prisoners. Unlike the majority of the Kudu inmates, Vanrennan and Graham had experienced at least a measure of freedom since the Japanese conquest of Malaya, only a matter of weeks earlier. They were soon turning their minds to the idea of 'escape'.

In the course of the military campaign in northern and central Malaya, upwards of 1000 British and Allied troops were taken prisoner. Those taken in northern Malaya were sent first to Taiping Gaol, while those from actions further south were held in Kudu Gaol, Kuala Lumpur. Within a short time all were joined together in very crowded quarters at Kudu. Gradually, the Kudu prisoners were moved south to the big POW camp at Changi, Singapore, or north to

Thailand for work on the Burma–Siam railway; rather more than 600 men went to Changi and about 400 to Thailand. All these moves took place between July 1942 and January 1943; meanwhile, about a month after the first contingent left for Singapore, on 17 July, a party of Kudu prisoners attempted an organised escape.

The escape organisation was formed in the cell of Lieutenants Vanrennan and Graham, both of whom, as mentioned, had been recently captured when operating with stay-behind parties. At first, there were two escape groups, another former 'stay-behind' officer joining Vanrennan and Graham, to make up the first one, and three other officers, Lieutenants Pelton, Salmon and Cubbit, making a second group. The senior British officer at the gaol was consulted. He agreed that it was the duty of the men to escape if they could, but thought it unlikely that they would get away from Malaya and felt that the Japanese would react harshly towards the rest of the prisoners, many of whom were suffering from beri-beri and dysentery. It was a difficult situation on which to seek advice and make a decision. Lieutenant Cubbit decided to resign from the escape organisation; the other officers became even more aware of the need for careful preparation to justify their attempt. They began to store food and other items.

Tinned food was accumulated when the Japanese allowed an outside dealer to supply the gaol canteen. Tools and materials for making keys were stolen by Vanrennan and Pelton, while on working parties in railway workshops and motor garages in the Kuala Lumpur area; quantities of hand grenades, explosives and small arms ammunition were also smuggled in from the same sources. Two sets of duplicate keys were made to fit three doors which would lead from the cells to freedom.

It was realised from the first that none of this type of preparation would, in itself, ensure success and that it would also be essential to enlist outside help. From March 1942 onwards, in the early weeks of the Japanese victory, Chinese civilians were brought into Kudu Gaol in large numbers, for interrogation purposes in the first instance. It was part of a wider policy of seeking out and punishing Chinese who were held to have been engaged in any kind of anti-Japanese activity. According to Lieutenant F. Pelton's detailed account of the escape operation at Kudu, conditions in the prison wing in which the Chinese were housed were 'indescribable'. There were six or eight to a cell, some died under questioning and dead bodies were often left for several hours. As some of the Chinese were released, fresh drafts were brought in.

Sometimes, it was possible to make limited contact, such as through a grille in a wall, with the Chinese prisoners, and Pelton befriended one, Chan Chin Chen, a newspaper proprietor whose family owned mining property at the village of Ampang on the outskirts of Kuala Lumpur. It was agreed between them that, on his release, Chan Chin would prepare a Chinese temple on the road from Ampang to Batu Caves, as a temporary refuge for escaped prisoners, and would maintain on-going contact from outside the gaol until the escape attempt had taken place.

By July, the number of potential escapers at Kudu had increased and preparations were complete, or almost so. Pelton was left on his own from one of the earlier groups, as Cubbit had withdrawn and Salmon became too ill to go ahead. There were three other small parties with a total of 13 men between them. Pelton's own plan (all the group plans had been discussed) was to rejoin the guerilla group of which he had been a member, and of whom five out of eight were still, to the best of his knowledge, at large. This meant hiding first, as arranged, at the Chinese temple, then heading south to the vicinity of Seremban. Before the agreed escape date arrived, however, the survivors of Pelton's former guerilla group were themselves brought into Kudu and imprisoned together in a cell in the gatehouse. They were in poor condition physically and their capture marked the end of Pelton's direct participation in the escape scheme. Another small group was persuaded to withdraw when one of its members became ill and further questions were raised with them about knowledge of the country and its languages.

This left 'Party 2', consisting of Harvey, Vanrennan and Graham, and Captains Hancock and Nugent, and 'Party 3', in which there was a Captain Macdonald, two army sergeants and a Dutch airman. 'Party 2' was to use the Chinese temple for cover for a few days, then make for previously known guerilla locations in Selangor, and perhaps further north in Perak. Beyond that, Captains Hancock and Nugent wanted to explore the possibilities of getting to India. 'Party 3' was to aim for the west coast of the Malay Peninsula, somewhere near to Port Dickson, try to secure a boat and plot an island-by-island crossing to Sumatra. Their eventual, and sadly optimistic, objective was to reach Australia.

One night, in the middle of August 1942, the main electric fuses in

Kudu Gaol were put out of order and the escape parties made their way out of the gaol in the ensuing darkness, according to plan. It had been previously agreed that all action would take place on the same night, and at the same time, but that, once out of the gaol, each of the two parties was free to act independently. The nine men succeeded in achieving the initial break-out and a number of British officers in the gaol were arrested and charged with complicity in the escape. All were sent to Singapore.

The two army sergeants reached Kajang, 14 miles south of Kuala Lumpur, and were picked up by a Japanese patrol there on the first night. After being held for two days, they were returned to Kudu, to be imprisoned together in a cell in the gatehouse. One of the captains was free for two days, then captured in Negri Sembilan, near the border with Malacca. Brought back to Kudu, he was taken for a time by the Japanese Military Police (Kempeitai) to their headquarters in Kuala Lumpur. Two of the lieutenants, Vanrennan and Nugent, were captured in a clash with Japanese troops near Karak, where Nugent was wounded. By the end of September, all the escapees were back in Kudu, locked in cells in the gatehouse.

Tragically, this was not the end of the affair. Under orders, it appears, from the Kempeitai, the re-captured escapees were soon taken out by lorry and driven, according to the Malaya lorry-driver, to a cemetery at Chevas, eight miles from Kuala Lumpur on the Seremban road. After a while, there were shots and the Japanese guards came back to the lorry with bundles of clothing. These were distributed in the gaol, where the Japanese commander claimed he did not know what had happened to the prisoners, as they were in the charge of the military police.

If an apparently well-planned escape of this kind, where some of the escapers were already familiar with jungle conditions and guerilla groups, could end in this way, it may well be asked what chance was there that any stray groups of cut-off or left-behind soldiers would fare better? Even from Kudu, the main hopes had been centred on reaching and joining the camps of jungle fighters, where a food supply and measure of protection might be found. The earlier view of the senior British officer at Kudu that it was unlikely that the escapers would get out of Malaya seemed fully justified and any plans for leaving Malaya had to be second-stage ones, usually left rather vague.

John Cross, a member of a small radio signals unit behind the Japanese lines in Johore, remembered that, in the weeks immedi-

ately following the fall of Singapore, there were early reports of
Europeans hiding in the Malayan jungle. Cross, with two other Royal
Signals men and a leader perhaps best described as an intelligence
officer, was already co-operating with Chinese Communist guerillas
when he heard of four Australians who had allegedly escaped from
Changi on 10 March, crossed to Pulau Ubin by boat and, with the
help of local Chinese, reached mainland Johore in another boat.
They were trekking in a west-north-west direction when they came
into contact with Chinese guerillas at Senai; this latter group was
already in touch with two other Australians, a lieutenant and a
corporal.

The six Australians now teamed up but they did not work happily
together, nor did they readily take advice and guidance from those
already established in the jungle. Unaided, the six men set off,
'making for Burma', but it was not long before they were captured by
the Japanese. Shortly after this, two more wandering groups were
identified in the Johore jungle. The first consisted of six Australian
privates and the second, a sizeable party of British and Australian
soldiers, numbered 15. The guerillas were willing enough at the time
to help military refugees like these and they supplied money, food
and medicine. But there was real security risk, especially where as
many as 20 or more were gathered together in the same place. Cross
tried to persuade some of his colleagues that, with Chinese help, the
soldiers could clear land and plant vegetables, making themselves
more self-supporting and perhaps helping the food-supply of the
guerillas as well. A few large guerilla camps did develop plantations
in jungle clearings but the idea was probably premature at that time
in Johore. In any case, Cross's party (known as 'Station A') and the
guerillas soon had much else to be concerned about, as their base was
suddenly attacked by a large number of Japanese troops and they
were forced to withdraw to the hills east of Kluang and set up a new
centre there.

Generally, matters did not improve for displaced soldiers, wandering in the jungle fringes. Many became weak and ill; all too often,
death followed quickly. Some were captured by Japanese patrols
and, if they were lucky, reached prison camps; some were shot. From
among such fugitive groups some accounts of successful escapes have
emerged, though only from a small minority. Certainly, the idea of
an escape was in the minds of many men who found themselves
trapped in such desperate circumstances. For many, escape from the
Peninsula started as their goal, but their attempts were only to end in
death or imprisonment.

In many places in the Malay Peninsula, fighting had taken place at close range and in situations which, at best, could be described as 'confused'. Troops often became dispersed in small groups along river banks or the jungle edge, becoming unaware of the location of the rest of their company, as well as uncertain about the disposition of enemy forces. This situation was heightened by the successful 'infiltration' tactics employed by units of the Japanese army and by a series of British withdrawals aimed at countering the use of pincer movements. British and Allied soldiers could find themselves in fierce engagements while in the process of a general withdrawal. This led at times to a search for cover and help in the jungle and for escape routes to the south, eventually to Singapore or other islands.

Some of the bitterest fighting in the Malayan Campaign took place in south-west Johore, from the banks of the River Muar southwards to Senggarang and Rengit, and inland along the line of roads to Yong Peng and Ayer Hitam. Much fighting took place around road blocks and in ambushes, and casualties were heavy in terrain where no one knew where the enemy would appear next. Large numbers of British troops were cut off at certain stages and, in what has sometimes been described as 'a miniature Dunkirk', the British navy mounted a rescue operation. HMS *Ping Wo*, normally a Chinese passenger and cargo boat, took off 650 troops from Batu Pahat on 29 January and, on the next day, HMS *Scorpion* rescued 2000 troops from Sungei Senggarang, 12 miles further south. Even as late as 3 February, with the Johore causeway already cut, two other ships, *Dragonfly* and *Shu Kwang*, picked up 90 members of the Indian Brigade at a pier in Johore, opposite to the Singapore naval base.

Prominent among the units which took the brunt of attacks from the Japanese Imperial Guards were a 'British Battalion', comprising men from the Leicesters and Surreys, the 2nd battalion of the Cambridgeshires and the 5th and 6th Battalions of the Royal Norfolk Regiment. There was also a Royal Artillery Field battery, a Field Ambulance unit and a Field Company of Royal Engineers. Australian and Indian forces were engaged at Muar and, subsequently, Australian positions lay generally inland from those manned by the British. In the close fighting in southern Johore, companies were split up, groups and individuals were cut off and men tried to make their way through swamp and jungle in attempts to link up again. For many, this was nothing less than a struggle for survival. Robert Hamond, in narrating the remarkable escape story of Private Jim Wright of the 6th Royal Norfolks (*A Fearful Freedom*) counted a total of 26 soldiers, 20 Australian and six British, who found their way into various jungle camps in southern Johore. There they lived for longer or shorter periods, only four of them surviving until the end of the war.

During the fighting in Johore, Company Sergeant-Major Melville Rudling, of the Norfolk Regiment, found that a Japanese advance which occurred on 25 and 26 January 1942, isolated the position of his battalion, positioned at that time between Rengit and Sengarrang. They were left to find their own way out to safety. Together with another sergeant-major, Rudling held a bren-gun post while most of the battalion withdrew. The two NCOs then followed. They soon caught up with other small groups of soldiers, some of them wounded, and all avoiding roads and making their way through swamp and jungle. There was a sharp encounter with a Japanese patrol, which caused further casualties, and the party then split up completely, Rudling being left with only two other men. By chance, they met two Australian soldiers, survivors of a party who had been captured and then machine-gunned. Left for dead under a pile of bodies, the two Australians had experienced a very lucky escape when their captors withdrew.

The five men sought food in Malay villages, where some were willing to help, but others were fearful of Japanese reprisals; villagers had to be aware at the same time that information about movements of British troops might be exacted under threats or worse. Reaching a wide, fast-flowing river, only Rudling and one of the Australians, who was wounded, chose to attempt to cross it, rather than turn back. The Australian did not make it, but was carried away by the current as Rudling reached the opposite bank, weak and exhausted. Making, as he thought, for the Johore coast, with a view to reaching Singapore, he stumbled on, losing sense of time and direction. Suddenly, he staggered straight into a hidden Japanese field-gun position, and was 'pounced upon'. As a rope was placed round his neck and his hands were tied, he thought he was going to be executed, but a Japanese medical officer, apparently attached to the field-gun unit, appeared and exchanged a few words in English with him. This may have relieved the situation of some tension and the Sergeant-Major was now treated with more consideration, though he could not know when the mood might change. So far as the military situation was concerned, he realised the worst had happened when he was taken across to Singapore island with the field-gun unit. One day, on the island, he was ordered to dig a trench, six feet deep, and about the length of his own body. He felt it could only be for his grave, especially as the Japanese soldier with him kept pointing a rifle at him and taking aim. In the end, it turned out the trench was intended to serve as a latrine. The CSM was left utterly exhausted, but, fortunately, there were no more incidents of this kind and he was eventually conveyed to Changi barracks as a prisoner-of-war.

An Australian sergeant, A. F. Shephard, of the 2/29th Battalion, 8th Australian Division, narrowly managed to avoid death or capture in the confused and close fighting in southern Malaya. In mid-January 1942, he was fighting the Japanese in a very tight situation at Bakri, near Muar. After being heavily engaged for three days, he and his men were ordered to withdraw a little over half a mile, to link up with reinforcements sent to reach them, but now themselves pinned down *en route*. After about 500 yards, a Japanese machine-gun nest opened up on them and caused heavy casualties. Ordered to make a detour round this, they ran into shell-fire from their own forces, which was being put down to cover their withdrawal. There were more casualties here and Shephard himself was wounded in the neck.

The survivors spent the night in a swamp, under machine-gun fire for much of the time, and made their way next day to a rubber plantation. Here, they came across a Chinese hut, where they were fed and rested. Sergeant Shephard and two others were left behind as they were 'in poor shape'. The Chinese (he was probably a woodcutter or charcoal burner) was given money to look after them and help them make their way towards Singapore when they were fit enough to do so. The three men hid in the swamp, but one (Gunner Brown) died after a few days and the other two, noting the agitated state of the Chinese as Japanese patrols were making frequent visits to the area, decided to move off, this time in a northerly direction. They faced the usual problems of finding food and help. At another Chinese dwelling, they were fed and led to a village where they were told to wait for a guide; he duly turned up, in the early of the next day, and led them to another village, where four British soldiers and two Australians were being sheltered. Five of the six were officers, one a former chief of police in Kedah, and the sixth man was a corporal.

At this stage of events, they picked up the news of the fall of Singapore and decided to keep on the move, especially as there was, understandably, some doubt about the lengths to which the local villagers would go to help them. This cruel dilemma affected both 'escapers' and those asked to help them, as even the smallest gestures of assistance were sufficient to put the lives of villagers at risk should the situation become known to the Japanese. Keeping to the jungle fringe, they encountered, a few days later, a Chinese who offered to guide them to a guerilla camp, an offer which they accepted willingly. They duly found a guerilla group in the early stages of organisation. Many men were engaged in picking up weapons from the battle areas and carrying them back to clean and repair. Companies and camps were being formed, each allocated an area to 'control'. Large and small camps were planned according to the possibilities of food-supply; some might eventually be able to support as many as 200, others as few as ten.

Sergeant Shephard spent the rest of the war period in guerilla camps. Frequently on the move at first, he became settled at what was to be known as the headquarters of the 4th Independent Company, north of Segamat, and just over the Pahang border. Here, his work included writing for a 'newspaper', printing money, drawing maps and training men in jungle warfare. Even in the better-situated and better-organised camps, life could still be dangerous and un-healthy. On three separate occasions, Shephard was so ill that the guerillas dug his grave, not expecting him to recover. Yet, at the end of the war, he came out of the jungle, near Segamat, and was quickly separated and sent home, a move which he thought was due to his having valuable information about the guerillas.

Shephard, known as 'Ah Shep' to the Chinese, had cheated death and avoided capture, but the death-toll among other British and Australian men whom he had met in the jungle was high. His original companion, one of the two with whom he had been left, 'in poor shape' at the first Chinese hut, died of beri-beri and malaria. A young British 2nd lieutenant died 'of some strange jungle disease' and an Australian private died from a combination of general weakness, beri-beri and malaria. At the guerilla headquarters, at different times, he heard of the deaths of four other British officers or NCOs whom he had encountered since taking to the jungle. When he finally left the camp and made for Segamat, he had, as companions, 'Doug' Stewart of the 2nd Battalion, Argyll and Sutherland Highlanders, and Maurice Cotterill, another rubber planter or, as was often the case, rubber-estate manager.

Douglas Broadhurst was a pre-war police officer in Malaya, stationed at Sungei Patani, then at Butterworth, opposite Penang. At the start of the Japanese invasion of Malaya he soon found himself in a front-line area and was very relieved that his wife, Marjorie, and their three children, could be quickly evacuated to the south. They reached Singapore safely and left on a Dutch ship on 31 December, making for South Africa. Meanwhile, as a member of the Volunteers, Broadhurst became engaged as liaison officer and interpreter, first to the 2nd Battalion, Argyll and Sutherland Highlanders, then to the 5th/2nd Punjab Regiment. In the course of the retreat to the south, he found himself behind the Japanese lines and in the company of two Argyll and Sutherland Highlanders, Gray and Gibson, who had recently been engaged in heavy, close-range fighting. Proceeding on foot through rubber estates and the jungle fringe, the three men were helped by both Malay and Chinese villagers who provided them with food and guides. Eventually, they reached Kampong Kuala Lukut, on the Selangor coast near Port Dickson. With Chinese help, they sailed out into the Malacca Strait, two weeks after the Johore causeway had been breached, and a day or so before the surrender of Singapore. Heading south, they landed first on Roepat Island and then made for the estuary of the Siak river in eastern Sumatra. They were still heading for Singapore, via Pulau Bengkalis, when they heard that the Japanese had been in control there for two days. Subsequently, they returned to Roepat and from there sailed again to the Siak river and travelled thence, via Pekan Baru, to Padang. Reporting to Brigadier Paris, the senior army officer there, they received the advice that Gray and Gibson should go to India and Broadhurst to Java, taking with them the useful information of their behind-the-lines experiences.

It was a fateful decision. Gray, Gibson and the brigadier left Padang, bound for Colombo, on the Dutch ship *Rooseboom*, and were torpedoed and sunk in the Indian Ocean. Only Gibson survived, and this only after the most horrendous experience in an open lifeboat, packed at first, and with many people holding on in the water, but eventually sheltering only Gibson, a Chinese girl and two Javanese, all close to death. Captured again on an island, Gibson was fiercely interrogated by the Japanese and held prisoner in Padang before being moved to Changi, Singapore. On this journey, he escaped death again after being torpedoed once more (but by the Allied side!) in the Malacca Strait.

Broadhurst's experience was different, but also adventurous. He reached Java from Padang and subsequently sailed from Tjiliatjap in southern Java to Australia. The ship was the fast liner *Zaandam*, and, by the standards of the time, the voyage was uneventful. Among those on board (and mentioned earlier) was 'Paddy' Martin, a rubber-estate manager from Johore, who made a late escape via the islands to the south and Sumatra. Martin's local knowledge of terrain and language had served him well as a liaison officer with the army and, before the end of the war, he was to serve again in Johore in 'special operations' and lose his life there. Douglas Broadhurst's experience in Malaya was also put to further use in 'special operations' in Japanese-occupied Timor and North Borneo and, eventually, once more in Malaya, where he was to witness the Japanese surrender. He had come, as it were, full circle.

Among others who sought and gained freedom, of a kind, in the Malayan jungle was Nona Baker, sister of Vincent, manager of the large tin mine at Sungei Lembing in Pahang. She had accompanied her brother and was with him when he died. Often ill and suffering greatly herself, she survived in Chinese guerilla camps and was free to return to England at the end of the war. J. K. Creer, a pre-war District Officer in Kelantan, also spent the years of the Japanese Occupation largely with guerillas in the jungle; most of those he lived with belonged to the Chinese Nationalist (Kuomintang) party, not the Malayan Communist Party. By 1945, these two organisations were almost at open war with each other. A handful of other Britons who stayed 'free' in a similar sense included game wardens, a forest officer and, until his death, allegedly at the hand of a Temiar, an anthropologist, Pat Noone. They 'escaped' in the sense that they were not killed or captured by the Japanese, nor did they linger in unhealthy prisoner-of-war or internment camps, or die a slow death under Japanese control on the Burma–Siam railway. But only a minority of those who took to the jungle for refuge and help managed to survive until the end of the war. Some were killed, more died of malnutrition and tropical disease; at least one, apparently moving towards madness, committed suicide. Over a long period of time, it became increasingly difficult for men to maintain that 'right mental attitude' which Spencer Chapman regarded as a necessary personal attribute for survival in the jungle.

A section of the 287th Field Company of the Royal Engineers was cut off at Senggarang in Johore when Japanese Imperial Guards, in effect, surrounded the village. Road blocks manned by Japanese machine-gunners barred the way to the south and, in an attempt made to open this up from Benut, further south, and relieve the troops at Sengga-rang, only one officer and one other rank got through. They reported that there were no less than eight Japanese road blocks between Senggarang and Benut. Wherever there was a patch of firm ground in the swampy territory on each side of the road, it was occupied by Japanese medium machine-guns. In what was to become known as the battle of Senggarang, after repeated attacks had failed to clear Japanese positions, the British troops eventually received orders to break out, using the jungle and making south.

Corporal Bob Tall's section of the Engineers had the specific task of blowing the Senggarang bridge and this was carried out by the section officer, Lieutenant P. A. D. Jones. The concentration of enemy road blocks to the south prompted a major decision to abandon all vehicles, destroying them first, and withdraw as many men as possible. This drastic order went out after many hours of fighting, and before darkness fell. The order, he recalled, was now 'every man for himself'; somehow the order passed round the scat-tered companies and sections. Sick and wounded soldiers who could not be moved were left in care of RAMC personnel and an army chaplain from the Cambridgeshires, Noel Duckworth.

Bob Tall, well equipped with compass, rifle, revolver, bag of grenades and, initially, a bren-gun, which he passed on to others, led a party inland into the jungle, where they trekked through the night, cutting a path as they went. He teamed up on the way with a friend, Sergeant Large, also leading a party out. Emerging on the line of the road, they found, *en route*, dead bodies of British soldiers, and collected their identity tags. They continued until they could see a road block ahead and movement round it. Sergeant Large, Corporal Tall and a soldier from the British Battalion who spoke Urdu went ahead to investigate. Bob Tall was challenged by a Japanese sentry, to whom he made a reply in German and gave a Nazi salute! Suddenly, he became aware of a machine-gun trained on him from the road block and of the presence of a considerable number (150–200, he estimated) of Japanese troops resting by the side of the road. The sentry motioned him to follow in that direction.

What happened next was, in Bob Tall's account, swift and dra-matic. The Japanese sentry turned to bring his rifle up, but Bob beat him to it and 'it all became a hornet's nest'. He felt the wind of bullets and part of his pack was shot away. He staggered to the side of the road with a wounded leg and a bayonet wound in his side. Meanwhile, he had 'put some grenades to good use' and he thought his rifle had 'become warm'. Rolling into a mud-hole on the jungle edge, he lay waiting and watching while the Japanese searched for him. His comrades, whom he had left to give covering fire, gave him up as dead, and scattered; he was, in due course, reported 'killed in action'. When it became dark, he started to crawl, his left leg paralysed. For the next six days, he was completely on his own, moving slowly and painfully along the ground and, as best he could judge, in the direction of the coast. He had left his water bottle with a comrade wounded by mortar shell on the bridge at Senggarang. How the young engineer survived this ordeal must still remain something of a mystery; his recollection was of finding 'the occasional coconut husk' and, when he finally reached the coast and found a sampan drawn up on the edge of the tide, of drinking the brackish water in the bottom of the boat, through a piece of rag.

He witnessed a Japanese landing, with a launch towing several sampans full of troops, then he set up a crude mast and sail, using sticks and his shirt and shorts, and floated the sampan on the tide. His last two grenades were used in an attempt to catch fish, the main result of which was damage to the bow-end of the sampan. The boat drifted along for several days until it came alongside a Chinese fisherman's hut on a sandbank. Two fishermen, Lim Sim Guan and Lim Pie, winched up the exhausted corporal in their fishing basket; there can be little doubt that they saved his life, as he had been without food and water for days. Their fishing hut proved a real sanctuary for him, giving him the chance to regain some strength. When a Chinese junk called to collect dried fish, he was able to sail with it to an island in the Malacca Strait, almost certainly Pulau Rangsang, at Tanjong Sampajang, where he met and was helped by the local Dutch Chief of Police. In a further crossing of the Strait, Bob Tall acted as bodyguard to some wealthy Chinese and reached Bengkalis, still closer to the Sumatran coast. Although nothing could be taken for granted, Corporal Tall was, for the time being, in a position of relative safety and poised to make a bid for freedom.

When sailing in the sampan he had taken off his socks for the first time in several days and the skin of his feet and lower part of his leg came with them. With a knife, he picked out the metal splinters from his leg and bathed it with sea water, as well as the wound in his side.

All this must have been excruciatingly painful, but his wounds became clean and gradually healed, though he would bear the scars for life. He was to acknowledge later that he had shown great will-power and sense of self-preservation and without these he would have been lost.

Reaching Pekan Baru in Sumatra, he picked up a lorry and drove two 'trigger-happy' Australians to Padang, where he found Lieutenant (later Captain) Fred Sibley, from his own RE Company, leading an escape party. They were, in the event, picked up by the destroyer, *Encounter*, and taken to Batavia. There followed a further long road journey southwards to the port of Tjiliatjap, where they boarded the Chinese river-steamer, *Wu Chang*, which is mentioned elsewhere. Sailing westwards through the Indian Ocean on 4 March, 1942, Lieutenant Sibley and Corporal Tall were among those who saw a Japanese submarine close to their ship and followed the track of two torpedoes which passed below them. It must have seemed that, after all that had happened, this was going to be the end. Sibley's reactions, however, were quick, as he hurriedly mounted a bamboo pole on the top deck to give the appearance of a gun. It may or may not have helped, but at least no further attack followed; on 8 March, they arrived at Colombo. It was still less than two months since 287th Field Company RE had first landed in Singapore. Among those who had survived death or imprisonment, none could have had a stranger experience than that of Bob Tall, who had answered the enemy sentry at the road block below Senggarang and, after much suffering and tribulation, 'got away with it'. But he was one of very few members of his Company who were not killed or taken prisoner, and many died on the Burma–Siam railway. After five months in Ceylon, he was evacuated by hospital ship to India, where he volunteered for Intelligence Special Duty Section work with explosives, later transferring to Intelligence Field Security. Over the years, several former comrades from Bob Tall's old Field Company were happily astonished to find that he had survived, eventually to live in retirement at Budleigh Salterton.

In a forced withdrawal from Johore, officers and men of the Royal Norfolks made for either the mainland west-coast or Singapore, where most became prisoners; only a few escaped. On the night of 13/14 February 1942, small parties of officers and men from a number of military units, including the Royal Norfolks, began to assemble at the Singapore waterfront. All they knew was that they had been selected and summoned for some kind of special operation or movement; now they learned that the plan was for naval vessels to come in and take them off; it was a last-minute military evacuation, but on a modest and selective scale. Each unit which received the message apparently determined the personnel, but not the number, in its own party, without really knowing what was afoot. Throughout the night Japanese shelling persisted spasmodically, the docks area remained highly dangerous and few, if any, troops were embarked. By morning, most of those waiting had moved to the YMCA building in Singapore to regroup and stay there in the hope of a possible further naval rescue mission the following night. A programme of departures was drawn up so that the re-organised group could move down to the docks in orderly fashion, and at intervals.

Events took a different turn. During the early evening of 14 February, a Japanese battery opened up and a number of shells scored direct hits on the YMCA building, causing casualties and confusion; among the scenes of damage and dead and wounded soldiers there was a natural movement to greater safety away from the building and the earlier plans for timed departures became meaningless. Instead, groups of soldiers wandered down to the waterfront and, before long, they were made aware that the time for naval rescues was now past. Rather, the instruction was to 'make your own arrangements and get off if you can'.

Remarkably, in the course of the night, and less than 24 hours before Singapore would be surrendered, some groups did get away in small boats. Captain Douglas Gray, of the 5th Royal Norfolks, searched the docks frantically until he found a large boat on a burnt-out ship. There was no lack of volunteers to man-handle this boat into the water and it took 35 men, with what provisions they could muster between them. With four oars working on either side they rowed out to the harbour entrance. By this time it was open daylight, but neither shot nor shell was fired at them. Japanese aircraft flew over twice, but nothing followed. The rowing was hard work, recorded Captain Gray, and half the men were sea-sick in the first hour, but 'we just kept on rowing and prayed for it to get dark'.

Their luck held. Despite striking a reef, the boat remained sea-worthy and they managed to rig up a makeshift red sail, possibly using a blanket. With the added movement and some rest from the rowing, they reached the island of Samboe and were able to hire a motorboat and crew to tow them across the Strait to the Sumatran coast. For reasons of security at the time, Captain Gray did not write down all the details of the voyage, but the boat was taken into an estuary where the escapers could seek further help. Gray calculated that, altogether, they had spent about three days in the boat before they were able to continue along a recognised escape route in Sumatra to the west coast port of Padang. Gray and probably most or all of that boatload from Singapore reached Ceylon, though for the Captain (later Major) tragedy lay in store; he was later killed in the fighting in Burma.

Lieutenant A. W. Nock, of the 6th Battalion, Royal Norfolk Regiment, found himself cut off, and in jungle swamp in Johore on 23 January 1942. He had an impression of moving round in circles, but tried to find a way eastwards to Ayer Hitam, a position he thought the British would still be holding. Walking at night and lying-up during the day, he rationed himself to three biscuits a day when he had finished a tin of bully beef. After four or five days of this, during which he had followed the course of a river inland as best he could, he came across a village, revealed himself and asked for food. There was some consternation at first, but he was helped, taken across the river and guided to a track which led to Ayer Hitam. Next day, he discovered that the nearest British-held position was at Benut, on the coast road and considerably to the south.

Nock had been on his own for most of a week when he met a party of eight soldiers from the Loyals who were also seeking a route to safety. Local villagers supplied them with food and advice and tried to direct them inland, away from the coast road which was said to be heavily used by the Japanese. Nock and his companions were seeking objectives which were fast disappearing. Giving up the idea of Benut, Nock came to think in terms of Johore Bahru, where he felt sure there would be a British stand until the Indian manager of a pineapple estate told him that only Singapore now lay outside Japanese control. This news called for a change of plan. They were a party of ten men, having collected another refugee in their wandering, and it was decided to split up into independent pairs. Even now, they met others in the same plight as themselves and Nock and his companion were joined by four Australians who decided to stay with them, making a new group of six.

A young English-speaking Malay in one of the villages now began to exercise a key influence on events for this group. Hiding close to the village of Sanglang, Nock began to raise with this young man the question of finding a sampan, making down-river to the sea and eventually crossing to Sumatra. The young Malay thought this would be much too far and too dangerous, but he referred the matter to an older man, whom he called his uncle, and from him the plan developed. The old man located a sampan ten miles down-river and had it provisioned with food and water and the means to light a fire for cooking. He also arranged to have new oars made for the boat. When all was said to be ready, the six men were instructed for a night trek to where the boat lay in a creek of the river. They had to cross the coast road at a village where Japanese were reported to be billeted, but all went well. They reached the boat, were helped to the bank by friendly Malays and were advised to handle the boat for about $1\frac{1}{2}$ miles, which would bring them to the estuary. There they were to lie up in a sidestream and row out on the tide the following night. As it appeared that no one of the six had any experience of rowing, it was an ambitious venture, to say the least.

In the darkness the water rose, first a dribble, then more like a flood. At 7.30 p.m. the boat was afloat and they rowed out into open water, making roughly south-west. It was 11 or 12 February, and in the distance they could see a burning Singapore. Appearing to make good headway, they passed several islands, a number of fish-traps and a lighthouse. 'We kept on till morning,' recorded Nock, 'rowing all out.'

But the next day was a very difficult one. They met a strong current and the sea became very choppy. For all their efforts they travelled in the wrong direction and, at 4 p.m. that afternoon, Nock, who had a map, calculated that they were opposite the mouth of the river at Batu Pahat, some 40 miles north of the point from where they had started. That night, utterly exhausted, the men could do no more than let the boat drift. Spirits were low and Nock saw their chances vanishing and believed they would all drown; the sooner, the better.

With daylight, they realised they had drifted out to sea again and the men were encouraged to row westwards again for most of the day. Another night of drifting brought them to the mangrove-fringed coastline of an island, and they pulled in. They were weary after 64 hours at sea and suffering from various ills, including sunburn and fever. The island was Bengkalis and they were close to the village of Montai, where friendly villagers looked after them, providing food and rest.

For the escapers, much travelling still lay ahead, but the worst was over. The old sampan was left high and dry on the mud and they were taken, after a short interval, to a place along the coast from where they could make overland to Bengkalis Town, the local centre of Dutch authority. The Dutch Controller and his wife looked after them and took under their care other small groups who arrived about the same time, by junk from Batu Pahat and sailing boat from Singapore. It was 16 February, and at 5 p.m. that afternoon Lieutenant Nock's group was taken by motor-launch to Pekan Baru in Sumatra. Two of the four Australians had fever and had to be left in hospital at separate times and places. Nock and the others reached Padang by lorry and Java on the British destroyer *Encounter*. They were now in a pattern of travel with many others. As they crossed Java from Batavia to Tjiliatjap, Nock was delighted to meet up again with members of the Royal Norfolks and the Cambridgeshires. It must have felt like coming home, and come home he did, for he survived the crossing of the Indian Ocean, on the *Wu Chang*, and survived the war too, to return to Norfolk life at Wymondham.

What comes through clearly from Nock's experience and that of others who were trapped in similar circumstances is the feeling of isolation and loneliness which they felt, away from their units and their comrades. It was a feeling, perhaps, not readily expressed in words, but a major cause of suffering in mind and spirit for the individual escaper.

Lieutenant (later Major) Barham Savory, an officer serving with the 5th Batallion Royal Norfolk Regiment, in a short, but hectic and violent period in southern Johore, wrote a contemporary account of the experience of breaking out from a situation of near-encirclement and heading south. Together with his men, he had received orders to take to the jungle on foot and find their way as best they could, first destroying any remaining troop-carriers they had. The battalion had landed at Singapore only some two weeks previously and had been 'pitched straight into it'. In close fighting they had suffered casualties and Savory had at one point been given up for dead; as he made for the jungle, he realised just how tired the members of his group were. They had been constantly 'on the go', with seldom more than two hours sleep at night and sometimes none at all. It was soon decided to lie up for the night in the jungle. A count revealed that the party numbered 13, under the Commanding Officer, Colonel Prattley, who, like Savory, was among the last to break out; a dog had also attached itself, seeking a measure of security in a frightening situation.

While others rested, three men took it in turns to keep watch during the night, an officer or sergeant and two others at a time. Early next morning, with the aid of a compass and a quarter-inch map, they attempted to make for the coast, facing the challenge of a swamp with a deep forest growing out of it. After four hours, they had made little progress and, coming across a deserted hut, they decided to lie up for a while. They were lucky to find water and a supply of coconuts here. There was also a more than welcome opportunity to take off boots and wash feet.

They set off again, changing course in an effort to make more progress. After about an hour, they came to a village, where the dog alarmed all the soldiers by spying some goats and chasing them, barking wildly. As the men tried to quieten the dog even more noise was created. Fortunately, this disturbance appeared to go unnoticed as the villages were mostly deserted and there would appear to have been no Japanese within earshot. There was little by way of military formation as they wandered on in single file, the officers going forward first when they appeared to be approaching anything suspicious.

After a while, they reached another village and met a Malay with whom the CO, having been in Malaya some 12 years earlier, could converse a little. This man was friendly and helpful and led them to a place on a river about a mile from the sea; equally valuable was his help in guiding them to a boat. Barham Savory felt he would have 'thought twice about using this to go up the Blakeney channel' (in north Norfolk), but one of his men, Private Smith, who hailed from Wells-next-the-Sea, pronounced the vessel seaworthy, provided the sea was calm! The boat, with six varied paddles, had to be carried about 500 yards and then deposited in an almost dry ditch, which, their Malay guide assured them, would fill up with the tide at 6 p.m. that evening, whereupon they could float down into the river and out with the tide. At the expected hour, the tide had not risen in the ditch, nor was there any significant change in the situation more than two hours later. Sentries who had been posted were reporting two men, dressed local-style, moving about the area, so it was decided to carry and drag the boat the remaining 300 yards or so to the river. They were only two or three miles from the main road and village which they knew were in Japanese hands. Having placed the boat in the river, all 13 men 'could just about fit in' and they floated down on the tide. For reasons unknown, this was the moment which the dog chose to abandon the party.

Having reached the sea without undue incident, they paddled all night and the next morning, one man keeping a foot on the leak in the bottom of the boat and baling out furiously with a tin hat and half a coconut shell. By mid-day, they were mostly out of drinking water and coconut juice and were all 'pretty well done up' and suffering from the heat of the day. They tried to make a landing, but this was immensely difficult on a coastline thick with mangroves and swamp and, in the end, they had to make their way to a river estuary and work hard to get the boat in against the outgoing tide. At a village close to the estuary they found two small parties of British troops who had arrived in sampans and were resting. Their news was that a British position had been withdrawn that morning from the next village up-river, so they filled their water-bottles and departed without delay. By now, the tide had turned and they had to fight their way against the incoming tide. As Barham Savory put it, the crew was also 'somewhat below the Henley standard'.

Reaching the sea at last, they tied the boat up to a hut on stilts over the water and rested in the hut for about two hours, having first eaten what remained of the bully beef and biscuits that they had been carrying. They set off again at 9 p.m. that evening and rowed until 2 a.m. By this time, despite the use of the compass, they found they were drifting in circles and they tied up at another hut over the water, keeping two men constantly on baling-out duty. At daylight, they were off again down the coast, and, about 9 a.m., they came in close to the shore, hoping they had reached a location still in British or Allied hands. They were cautious about making or identifying any signal, and not re-assured when someone on land fired a rifle. But a shout from an English voice followed (it was a Royal Artillery officer who called) and they landed to meet friendly help. Left to itself, the water 'gurgled up through the leak in the boat' and it was not going to be long before the vessel sank. But, difficult as it had been to handle, the boat had served them well, by-passing advanced enemy posts and allowing, in the end, access to the road by which they were to make a final withdrawal from the mainland to Singapore. Their very memorable boat journey had taken them from south-east of Senggarang to Pontian Kechil and a route to Singapore. Some two weeks later, Savory was a member of the official military evacuation party and, though this move collapsed, he did get away, through other adventures, to Sumatra, Java and Ceylon. He was very conscious of his great good luck. But, then, there was no way of telling which way the wheel of fortune would turn for any evacuee or escaper.

Select Bibliography

UNPUBLISHED SOURCES

Personal Correspondence from:

Mrs A. Apthorp
Col. M. B. H. Ashmore
Wing Cdr W. S. Brereton Martin
Dr T. C. Carter
Mrs P. Christie
Mrs M. F. Colley
Capt. M. J. Curtis
Mr J. O. Dykes
Mr I. Finlay
Mrs E. E. T. Garnons Williams
Mrs C. Goodfellow
Mrs D. E. Gurney
Maj. R. Hamond
Vice-Admiral Sir John Hayes
Mrs F. Hosking
Miss N. Inge
Mrs E. Innes Ker
Mme M. A. de Jonge
Mr R. G. Jackson
Mr W. B. Johnson
Wing Cdr P. N. Kingwill
Mrs S. Lea (née Brown)
Mrs M. de Malmanche

Dr J. Marsh
Mrs O. Moffatt
A. W. Nock family
Mr M. Ogle
Mrs B. Parnell
Mr G. Patterson
Mrs R. Ramsay Rae
Mr J. T. Rea
Mrs M. Reilly
Lt-Col. D. Russell-Roberts
Maj. Barham Savory
Mr P. Sothcott
Mrs K. Stapledon
Mr C. D. Stenton
Mrs P. Stevens
Mrs E. Stevenson (née Wood)
Mr Bob Tall
Mrs P. Thorn (née Briggs)
Miss M. Thomas
Mr H. C. Vanburen
Mrs P. Wallwork
Mr A. J. Willis
Lt-Col. G. P. Wood

Private Papers in Deposit at Rhodes House Library, Oxford (MS Indian Ocean series)

Cardew, A. H. P.	Letter and Report, 1942	MSS Ind Ocn s90
Clarke, Mrs F. F.	Malayan Diary, 1942	MSS Ind Ocn s116
Coupland, Miss J.	Diaries, Palembang, 1942–4	MSS Ind Ocn r9
Davis, R. P.	Diary, Malaya, 1941–2	MSS Ind Ocn s33
Denny, Capt. J. R. C.	Diary, Malaya, 1941–2	MSS Ind Ocn s227(1)

Geake, F. H.	Diary, Singapore, 1942–5	MSS Ind Ocn s219–22
Gorsuch, L. H.	'Crooked Figure' (autobiographical, Malaya, 1940–5)	MSS Ind Ocn s91
Hardman, J.	Singapore and Penang Harbour Board, Report, 1942	MSS Ind Ocn s29
Husband, T. G.	Narrative of Escape, 1942	MSS Ind Ocn s211
Lacey, Miss H. G.	Diary, Malaya, 1942	MSS Ind Ocn r8
McPherson, Miss D. R.	Seremban Hospital – report, 1942	MSS Ind Ocn s132
Niven, A. and Niven, Mrs E. (née Mills)	Personal letters, 1942–5	MSS Ind Ocn s98 MSS Ind Ocn s99
Ogle, M.	Escape from Singapore, 1942	MSS Ind Ocn s173
O'Grady, G. J.	Life in Malaya, 1928–42	MSS Ind Ocn r6
Wegener, W. F.	Report on Evacuation, Malaya, 1942	MSS Ind Ocn s50

Private Papers in Deposit at the Imperial War Museum, London

Ashmore, Col. B. H.	(in Percival Papers) Singapore to Colombo, 1942
Briggs, Miss P. M. (later, Mrs Thorn)	Experiences of nursing sister, Malaya and Singapore, 1941–2
Brown, Miss S. D. (later Mrs Lea)	Experiences, Singapore and Sumatra, 1942–5
Carter, Dr T. C. Sqdn Leader, later Wing Cdr	Papers on RAF radar, Malaya and Singapore, and own experience, Singapore to Ceylon, 1942
Colley, Mrs M. F.	Diaries, Sumatra, 1942–5
Dillon, Lt-Col F. J.	Personal records and account, Singapore, Sumatra, Thailand, 1942–5
Dykes, Ft/Lt J. O.	(in T. C. Carter Papers) Escape, Singapore – Sumatra, Burma
Dodds, F/O R. D.	Diary, HMS Trang (and afterwards) from Singapore, 1942

Fukuda, K. — Diary, 1941–2, Japanese internee

Garnons Williams, Capt G. A. — Collected papers and reports of British personnel left behind or landed in Malaya, 1941–5

Goodfellow, Surg. Cdr D. R. — Reports, including voyage of *Empress of Japan*, 1942

Hosking, Maj. E. C. — Stories of the Malayan Campaign

Howell, Mrs G. — Letters, especially in relation to husband, Charles, former Attorney-General, Singapore, and to escape story of W. R. Reynolds, 1942

Inge, Miss N. — Autobiographical account, especially bearing on Japanese internees, 1941–6

Innes Ker, Mrs E. — Autobiographical account, 1939–45, especially evacuation Singapore–Java–Australia

Johnson, Lt W. J. B. — Letters, 1940–2, especially relating to escape experiences, Singapore–Sumatra–Ceylon, 1942

de Jong, Mme M. A. — Account of life in Java, 1937–45

de Malmanche, Mrs M. — Account, Singapore and Sumatra, 1942–5

Marsh, Maj. J. W. P. — Experiences, Singapore, Sumatra, Thailand, 1942–5

Moffat, Mrs O. S. — Letter describing experiences, Malaya, Singapore and evacuation to Australia, 1941–2

Pelton, Ft/Lt F. D.
Pelton, Mrs D. — Letters, 1941–5, especially related to Mrs Pelton's evacuation from Singapore and Ft/Lt Pelton's account of a prison escape attempt, Malaya, 1942

Ramsay Rae, Wing Cdr A. — Collected Papers include lists of British internees in various Japanese prison camps, 1942–5

Reilly, Mrs M. M. — Experiences, 1941–2, including evacuation, Singapore–Java and, subsequently, Australia

Rudling, Sgt Maj. M. E. — Escape and recapture, Malaya, Singapore, 1941–2

Shephard, Sgt A. F. — Escape and life in Malayan jungle, mainly 1941–2

Stapledon, Mrs K.	Evacuation, Singapore to Australia, and, subsequently, England, 1941–2
Stevenson, Mrs E. (*née* Wood)	Autobiography: special reference to experiences, Singapore–Sumatra–Ceylon, 1941–2
Willis, Sgt A. J.	Autobiography

Private Papers in Deposit at the Royal Commonwealth Society Library, London

M. C. Hay

Archives Held at Naval Historical Records Branch, London

Singapore, 1942 (3 vols)
Singapore Chronology
Survivors' Reports

On Loan, Pre-publication, from Mrs Ann Apthorp

Apthorp, Maj. Desmond P., 'British Battalion Diary, 1942–45'

Letters Held by Major Robert Hamond

Douglas Gray
Barham Savory

PUBLISHED SOURCES

Books and Articles

ATTIWILL, KENNETH, *The Singapore Story* (Frederick Muller, 1959).
BARBER, NOEL, *Sinister Twilight* (Collins, 1968).
BEHRENS, C. B. A., *Merchant Shipping and the Demands of War*, History of the Second World War, UK Civil Series, ed. Sir Keith Hancock (HMSO, 1955).
BROOKE, Lt-Cdr GEOFFREY, *Alarm Starboard* (Patrick Stephens, 1982).
CALLAHAN, RAYMOND, *The Worst Disaster* (University of Delaware Press, 1977).
CHAPMAN, F. SPENCER, *The Jungle is Neutral* (Chatto & Windus, 1949).
COLLIER, BASIL, *The War in the Far East* (Heinemann, 1969).
CROSS, JOHN, *Red Jungle* (Robert Hale, 1975).
CUNYNGHAM-BROWN, J. S. H., *Crowded Hour* (John Murray, 1975).
FALK, STANLEY, *70 Days of Singapore* (Robert Hale, 1975).

GIBSON, WALTER, *The Boat* (W. H. Allen, 1952).
GILMOUR, OSWALD W., *Singapore to Freedom* (Ed. J. Burrow & Co., 1943).
GORDON, ERNEST, *Miracle on the River Kwai* (Collins, 1963).
GORDON-BENNETT, Maj.-Gen. H., *Why Singapore Fell* (Angus & Robertson, 1944).
GOUGH, RICHARD, *The Escape from Singapore* (William Kimber, 1987).
HALL, TIMOTHY, *The Fall of Singapore* (Methuen, Australia, 1983).
HAMOND, ROBERT, *A Fearful Freedom* (Leo Cooper, 1984).
HOLMAN, DENNIS, *Noone of the Ulu* (Heinemann, 1958).
HOLMAN, DENNIS, *Green Torture* (Robert Hale, 1962).
HOLMES, RICHARD and KEMP, ANTHONY, *The Bitter End* (Anthony Bird, 1982).
JENNINGS, C. O., *An Ocean without Shores* (Hodder & Stoughton, 1950).
JEFFREY, BETTY, *White Coolies* (Angus & Robertson, 1954).
KENNEDY, JOSEPH, *British Civilians and the Japanese War in Malaya and Singapore, 1941–45* (Macmillan, 1987).
LEASOR, JAMES, *Singapore: The Battle that Changed the World* (Hodder & Stoughton, 1968).
LIM, JANET, *Sold for Silver* (Collins, 1958).
McCORMAC, CHARLES, *You'll Die in Singapore* (Robert Hale, 1954).
McDOUGALL, WILLIAM, H., *By Eastern Windows* (Arthur Barker, 1951).
McINTYRE, W. D., 'The Strategic Importance of Singapore, 1917–1942', *Journal of South·East Asian Studies*, vol. X, no. 1 (March 1969).
TIERNEY, JANE, *Tobo* (Piatkus, 1988).
The Times, 'The Tragic Islands', 17 June 1942.
TSUJI, M., *Singapore: The Japanese Version* (Constable, 1962).
WILLMOTT, H. A., *Empires in the Balance* (Orbis Publishing, 1982).
WOODBURN-KIRBY, Maj.-Gen. S., *History of the Second World War: The War Against Japan*, vol. 1 (HMSO, 1957).
WOODBURN-KIRBY, Maj.-Gen. S., *Singapore: The Chain of Disaster* (Cassell, 1971).

Index